Hothead

Hothead

a poem

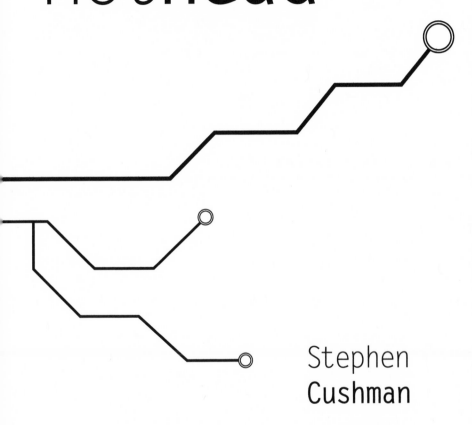

Stephen
Cushman

LOUISIANA STATE UNIVERSITY PRESS   Baton Rouge

Publication of this book made possible in part by the Buckner W. Clay Dean of Arts and Sciences and the Vice Provost for Research, University of Virginia.

Published by Louisiana State University Press
Copyright © 2018 by Stephen Cushman

DESIGNER: *Mandy McDonald Scallan*
TYPEFACE: *Sina Nova*
PRINTER AND BINDER: *Sheridan Books*

Grateful thanks are due to Stephan Delbos, editor of *B O D Y* (Prague), and Caleb Caldwell, editor of *The Spectacle,* for printing portions of this poem.

Library of Congress Cataloging-in-Publication Data
Names: Cushman, Stephen, 1956– author.
Title: Hothead : a poem / Stephen Cushman.
Description: Baton Rouge : Louisiana State University Press, [2018] | "LSU
    Press Paperback Original"—Title page verso.
Identifiers: LCCN 2017038112| ISBN 978-0-8071-6782-3 (pbk. : alk. paper) | ISBN
    978-0-8071-6783-0 (pdf) | ISBN 978-0-8071-6784-7 (epub)
Classification: LCC PS3553.U745 A6 2018 | DDC 811/.54—dc23
LC record available at https://lccn.loc.gov/2017038112

Hothead

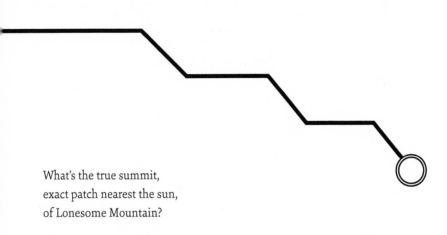

What's the true summit,
exact patch nearest the sun,
of Lonesome Mountain?

Flip-flop, tick-tock, ding-dong, everybody sing along,
criss-cross, hip-hop, ping pong, that's the way, now with *a,*
chit-chat, dilly-dally, shilly-shally, keep the beat,
flim-flam, pitter-patter, riff-raff, sure, they duplicate
but more than that they shift the airflow back or down
in your marvelous mouth, that breeding pool for lots of germs,
wet and warm, the primal swamp, and better watch out,
floss and brush, rinse and spit, or many bad things, thrush
or cankers, trench mouth, cold sores, herpes, gum disease,
can really cut down on oral pleasure, but oh that pleasure,
anal and genital, late to the dance, can never surpass
the joyous agenda always attending the tip of the tongue,
flexible bundle of muscles extending off the mouth floor
out through lips toward someone else or in through lips
toward someone else, no way, can't hold a candle,
someone I know can hold a candle, prefers the scented,
but don't expect any descriptors from me, no sirree,
no pronouns either, make the picture work for you,
as for pleasures the oral affords, the ice cream thing
is lost on me, nice big bowl of sweet cold fat,
but others' pleasure can give much pleasure, here's a kid

smearing his face with a double-scoop cone, can't keep up
with its melt in the sun, or a gaggle of girls intently licking,
eyes on each others' with looks that say, It doesn't get better,
they may well be right, sad to think so, some will find out,
or a vast St. Bernard enjoying a dish of vanilla with sprinkles,
and that's just food, the original intake, okay the latecomers
can take in too, give them their due, while as for output
there's really no contest, puking's no picnic and spitting's good
if you've coughed up phlegm or chew tobacco or suddenly hanker
to demonstrate scorn, but on the ladder to pleasures superlative
these delights show fear of heights, there's always drinking,
also smoking, but the big one, face it, is the pleasure of speaking,
what can compete with orality, nothing, no one's saying
writing's subordinate or merely transcription of a spoken supreme,
down deconstructors, but when you read or write things down,
the brain's mirror neurons deliver small pulses straight to the mouth,
so reading and writing both diddle the oral, whatever their status
in another ontology, but all of this is way off-track,
not at all pertinent to what's on my mind.

Stand clear of the doors.
Digression's not a sidetrack.
It's a faster train.

Shit-show, reduplicant, that's how it started, though shit-shot's the one
in line with above, yet shit-show still follows the vocalic pattern
of tense to lax, and that's where it's at, first you get tense, then you relax,
ease the jaw lower to manage that *o,* tense then relax, the primary paradigm
for, for example, sex in most movies and knockoffs at home, get all that
        tension
over with fast, why would one possibly want it to last,
coiled Kundalini climbing the spine, slowly, for hours, sit or lie still
instead of that rabbit thing, breathe in in unison, or as one mate inhales
the other exhales, hold both her eyes, or his eyes, with yours,
and try out some mantras, *lam* and *vam, ram, yam, bam, om,* sounds

without meaning, simple vibrations for piercing the chakras, you may
start to shake, that's just the energy, but who wants to dawdle
when thrusting and pounding can leave lots of bruises, even draw blood,
generate infections, and suddenly it's over, gee, that was great, maybe a nap,
and you're both good to go, but soon it's the shit-show starting again,
the building of tension, the need for release, but the shit-show I started with
wasn't the sex one, it's the election, six weeks away, no seven I checked,
conventions all done, talk about shit-shows, debates still to come,
and then in the meantime it's death-by-paid-ad, safer to smoke
three packs a day, Camels, no filters, than take in that stuff,
though on our heads be it if we turn away, put on the smug mug,
dismiss the whole thing and say it won't matter, they're both
money puppets or sellouts or scumbags, you choose the putdown,
elections are farces, distractions for masses, add for good measure,
and forget or write off the election of Lincoln, bye-bye Carolina,
South the next month, but North followed too, and next thing you know
it's four years of averaging, each day this is, six hundred dead,
yesterday Antietam, big anniversary, or you can say Sharpsburg,
and isn't this spooky, this year election day's set for the sixth,
same day it was in that drastic year, one thing's for sure, if it rains hard
as it's raining today, turnout won't help whoever most needs it.

This very minute
it's cataract surgery
for my one-eyed mom.

Lincoln didn't carry a single southern state, not forty percent
of the popular vote, three other candidates, can we still name them,
Douglas okay, you know the debates, but what about Breckenridge,
came from Kentucky, Buchanan's vice president, during the war
the general who led, at the Field of Shoes, cadet adolescents,
and then there was Bell, carried three states, and his running mate,
Everett, who spoke for two hours before Lincoln at Gettysburg,
and here, this is interesting, first they'll anesthetize the eye,
and that means a needle in the vicinity, here this is interesting,

earlier Everett was president of Harvard and the thirteen percent
he garnered with Bell came mostly from the South, ironies, ironies,
a decade of ironies, the question now, after it's over, allow three hours,
she'll wear a shield with holes for light, something like a tea-strainer,
the question now, is irony dead, first it was God, but now is it irony,
Douglas came second in popular vote but won one lone state
to Lincoln's eighteen, eleven for Breckenridge, Missouri he won,
tsk, tsk, how ironic, right about now anesthesia's taking hold,
but just what is irony, a luxury of hindsight, or is it class privilege,
a taste acquired, like coffee or absinthe, or what's that Italian stuff,
Fernet Branca, last time I drank it, great bar in North Beach,
bartender chuckled, nobody'd asked for that bottle in ages,
bitter, man, bitter, tastes like a medicine made from old mud
and lots of crushed herbs, recipe's a secret since 1845, same year
Mary Lincoln got pregnant with Eddie, who died shy of four,
ten months before Willie was born, ironic you say, but no it's not irony,
it's simply coincidence, for which it's mistaken, irony that is,
as some kind of synonym, or maybe not coincidence but larger
congruence in the eyes, or the eye, here comes the laser,
there goes the lens, in the eye that still sees, pace Nietzsche,
something that science cannot account for, something not wholly
of one's own invention, something beginning where knowledge dead-ends
as knowledge always will, no matter how much it happens to grow,
bitter, a taste it helps to acquire, if given a choice, pass
on the irony and go for the bitterness, don't become bitter, that's not
what it takes, but learn to like bitter and you're set for life,
set for death too, or at least for the dying, is there a secret, usually there is,
in this case the distillery slyly admits to twenty-seven herbs
from four different continents, among them aloe, gentian root,
rhubarb, gum myrrh, red cinchona bark, galangal, what's galangal,
and something called zedoary, have to look them up, she used to be
a reference librarian, look it up she'd say, at first we resent it,
precious time lost, reading rate ruptured, stomping the stairs
to find the damn dictionary, but then through the years slowly a change,
slowly the reading without looking up becomes as unthinkable

as love without touch, both come from Asia and have names that passed
from China or Persia through Arabic to Latin, maybe Old French,
and into Middle English, did Chaucer know the stuff, watch the word travel
the Silk Road beat, trade routes across the Indian Ocean, globalism new,
you've got to be kidding, she's been there two hours, probably now
they're cleaning her up, starting to ready the shield for fitting,
her one window shuttered against the harsh light.

It's almost autumn,
stupefying butterfly.
Too late to love you.

Today's crispy blue, tomorrow's Yom Kippur, or really this evening
at 7:05, sunset and sunrise differ by a minute, makes perfect sense
to start a new year this time of year, Romans looked to March
to kick it all off, that would do too, but January, cut the crap,
it takes imagination, even on a good day, to breathe deep renewal
but throw in flu season, and you've got a challenge, happy nose-blowing,
happy cold snap, happy black ice, happy skidding off into a drift,
happy snow-shoveling, happy heating bills, happy hooded mornings,
seems a better time to yank all the plugs and crawl into bed
till maybe late February, first crocus coming, but the autumn option,
never really thought about it, best time of year and something to be said
for sublime decline as true inauguration, confession, check, know about that
and also atonement, but the best thing about Yamim Nora'im,
at least from the outside, looks like the granting of one last extension,
ten days of amnesty during gorgeous weather, before your fate's final,
a clear sunny grace period, low-humidity loophole, Calvin missed the boat
or set out to sink it, if you're predestined, nothing you can do,
where's the incentive, what keeps you trying or even barely cheerful,
but give me a chance to stave off the F, you bet I'm going to try,
cue up the cricket track, days in the 70s, windows cranked wide
and nights built for blankets, in many too many New Testament circles
I AM THAT I AM gets a bad rap, as though after Malachi
suddenly a makeover, love is discovered, along with forgiveness,

but that isn't right, in Egypt, in Sumer, in dark scarlet Babylon
hymns sang the mercy that comes with divinity, today visibility
over ten miles, barometer steady, one of the terms in Hebrew for mercy
derives from the word for uterus, gentlemen.

To haves and have-nots
let's add the category
hads-who-had-had-it.

Sometimes a face is helping one face it, may it be so you know one of those
shining your way when nothing else does, but the Big Face, that's tough,
scripture mixes signals, and Whitman's glib dictum, re contradiction,
doesn't help much in cases when faces you see could destroy you
faster than Medusa or basilisk halitosis, says right here
You cannot see my face and live, Dickinson quoted that one too,
but nine verses earlier there's face-to-face speaking, as someone speaks
to closest friends, inside the tent, or here in this psalm, Seek ye my face,
Thy face do I seek, Hide not thy face from me, is it a death wish
one has to have to sing such a thing, is there a fundamentalist
somewhere in the house, there's a word that's been treated badly,
worse than most who do the complaining, what could be wrong
with love of the fundament, the buttocks, the anus, the natural features
of a land surface altered by no human being, primary definitions,
checked three dictionaries, none of them online, and what do you make
of Exodus 33, right at the end, when Moses gets a glimpse
of divine backside, sometimes it's tricky, reverence and heresy
can sound very similar, and when does the former in some ears
cross over and turn into blasphemy, deserving of brimstone,
this is not blasphemy, it's the drive to get down to the bottom of things,
the basics, foundation, faces are fine, but can you trust faces
in a country that spends so much on cosmetics, don't get me wrong,
I love a good painting, Manet's *Dead Toreador* hangs in this room
and in the hall *Guernica,* no reason why the painting of eyes,
cheeks, lips, or nails has to be censured, if your body's a canvas
bring on the palette, but divinity's face, should it wear makeup,
is that what we're seeking, Job saw the face, 42:5, is that what it takes,

you have to lose everything, or did he see otherwise, the Almighty
buttocks mooning him big time, not necessarily a gesture of scorn
except to self-righteousness Job was not free of, the moment you say
why me you're toast, then the moon flashes, but find a way somehow
to say it's my turn, everybody takes one, this one is mine,
and then there's the face, unpainted, eye contact,
another good book is Esther, who's gutsy.

Enheduanna,
the first non-anonymous
poet known to us.

Here's the puzzle, priestess of Ishtar, daughter of Sargon,
emperor of Ur, or whatever they called him in southeast Iraq,
whether you're hymning a goddess on tablets, in lines of cuneiform
cut in two columns, before the clay dries, or rattling away
on some aging keyboard five more millennia farther down the chute,
no song without rhythm, no rhythm sans pattern, but when does a pattern
run into rut, what goes for lines goes double for lives, Tuesday again
and once again raining, how does it know, and who does the knowing,
is it the weather that's tracking our week, or does the god Tiu
we got from the Norse, boss of the sky, also of war, say my day again,
bring on the rain, irony there, not a good war day, hard day to march
or land or bomb, rivers rising high, cloud ceiling low, feel the squeeze
of the soggy sandwich, lots of wet Tuesdays during this stretch,
call it coincidence 'cause that's what it is, the slow coinciding
of two separate rhythms, usually oblivious to the other's operation
but for a short interval exactly aligned, that's when things happen,
when rhythms enmesh, one mounts the other, whether it's weather
or cuneiform columns or the other coinciding as I go inside
the temple of you, want a guided tour, every hour on the hour,
no thanks, I know my way around, but I'm happy to leave
a small donation, sure, it's repetition if we've interlocked before,
and all repetition's risking a rut, or sometimes one's rhythm
goes off on its own, the other's unaligned, not a catastrophe,
let it push through to pleasured conclusion, but if the two rhythms

should finally combine, nobody leading, everybody follows,
good golly miss molly, watch the fuse blow, suddenly ruts risked
repay with rich rutting, two Tuesdays ago it also rained hard
but with lots of wind that sent branches snapping, limbs on the ridge
swinging like pendula Poe could make hay with, not a smart day
to hike up the mountain, but the danger was thrilling, everything thrashing,
lots of it dropping, not very prudent, I have no excuse,
more acorns falling than I've seen before.

Syntax is sexy.
Consider the copula
and this conjunction.

Maruirui, what does it mean in Kiswahili, party hard in Zanzibar
you'll know soon enough, a word for hangover tells one a lot
about a language distressed heads hurt in, electrolytes lost, tummies a mess,
how many languages Hemingway drank in, there's a topic one can suggest
the next time they whine what's there to write about, much more interesting
than did she get laid is whether Ms. Dickinson wrote with a hangover, if so,
how often, maybe a theory for some of those dashes, she made wine jelly,
can't do that unless you've got wine, tough to get the recipe right
unless you taste it, one thing, it seems, leads to another, you can't get tight
on air or dew unless you know what tight is, Whitman, sure,
loved to get loaded, now for the superstars, Lowry in Mexico,
Kerouac anywhere, bad-ass Bukowski, who pointed out rightly
it takes strength to drink, Williams didn't have it, gave it a try,
but lacked the constitution both to go boozing and see all those patients
at dawn or at midnight, it's a dark matter, this matter of enhancing
how we perform with various substances, or how we come down
from performing we've done, even Lord Jesus had to go off, pound down
that solitude, he drank too, in Cana, hell, he changed enough water
to keep the party going another two months, everybody knee-walking,
do the math, six stone jars, twenty or thirty gallons apiece, all very well
to say he's your savior, but do the math, excess, excess, Blake is right,
it's not just the road, it's the multilane interstate, if not to the palace
then the rest stop of wisdom, but excess isn't the only road,

ask an anorexic, unless that's excess in cross-dressed get-up,
it's a dark matter, the line that divides ascetics from addicts,
drinking responsibly, what a weird phrase, thanks so much
for the kind invitation, afraid I can't make it, too many responsibilities,
drinking among them, but if you can manage to get through somehow
without immoderate moderation, tepid oatmeal, mediocre tapioca,
you and your muse, espoused all these years, are just plain old enough,
if not to know better, at least to appreciate each other's infirmity,
sure, it was great back when you could say What in me is dark
Illumine, and just like that, she'd come and go down, or make it a he
you used to invoke, but let's stick with she for this illustration,
she would do anything with first-rate technique, but now it's so nice
to rock by the fire, watching her knit, a line at a time, long rows
of phrases, knit one, purl one, there in her bathrobe, comfortable slippers,
bifocals, chatting, no answer needed, she does like to talk,
patter away, the weather for instance, another blue day,
high sixties, October, leaves snapping on, she understands
if you nod off, she'll be there still talking whenever you wake,
what was that, honey, did you say dark matter, twelve years ago
someone discovered twenty-three percent of the visible universe
consists of dark matter, throw in, for dark energy, seventy-three more
and here's your change, mister, the visible universe we love and we praise
a mere four percent of what there is out there, a mere four percent,
and here Einstein scoffs, in a letter just auctioned, yours for three million,
at childish stories contained in the Bible, saying instead his only religion's
the structure of the universe, now there's a big Duh, so much for genius,
a child asks where babies come from, you say the stork, that's pretty
childish, but childish or not, it doesn't mean there's no reproduction.

If beauty can kill,
October assassinates,
high-powered hit-month.

Feast of James today, not the son of Zebedee, who fished the Sea of Galilee,
shindig for him's not till July, best in Santiago, in lisping Galithia,
pero cuidado, es peligroso, o puede ser, vaulting bonfires after wine,

try the Albarino, this gringo machine won't make an *enya*, met a *senorita,*
era muy bonita, who'd stalled in mid-vault, legs got it bad, third-degree
monstrosities, medication mitigating ongoing agony, skin-grafts to come,
celebration's riskiness may explain why it's so awfully rare, safer to answer
pollsters who call with stern disapproval, safer to say hell no I ain't satisfied
than sail out today and fall on stiff knees at the sight of the sky
like Kit Smart in Hyde Park, danger, danger, there she blows again,
got blue eyes, put on shades, otherwise cataracts will soon play the scales
clouding your future, a friendly optometrist will peek in those bulbs
and say they're not clear, one must be careful with praying for radiance,
there you go intoning what's dark in me illumine, when bang it happens,
somehow the switch suddenly flicks on and now you're blinking
nearly blind, colors start fading, night-driving's out, how does this happen,
each time I come here I've got stuff to say, brought an outline today
and meant to admit to struggling with hatred for undecided voters,
wanted to think about wandering hominids steering to Sumer,
and really really hoped to chat about the Daddy Longlegs
emerging in legions this time of year, an order of arachnids
also called harvestmen, makes sense, it's harvest time, harvest moon
will be full soon, but they're not spiders, haven't got venom glands,
and boy are they friendly, crawl all over you, climb up the hand
holding down a page, next thing you know it's up the steep ascent
to shoulder and neck, they like the hair too, these guys are ancient,
been around, fossils show, since the Devonian, how can they be so trusting,
if people swatted them, descent with modification would surely mean
they'd be much better at evasive action, so it must be the case
we've treated them well, how could you not, forelegs tickling
the skin right nicely, but it didn't happen, opened a book,
found James's feast day, and look at this mess, is this what the young,
attentions deficient, struggle with always, metonymy gone mad,
contagious contiguity, where can one turn to pull it together
when there's the rapist hiding in therapist, notice me, notice me
everything's shouting, and then, should you notice, everything's interesting,
if attention were money, this would be spendthrift, but today I'm determined
and will see it through, something at least, let's make it James,

the teacher's little brother who while his brother lived, gospels all agree,
wasn't much impressed, but then the Resurrection, his brother paid a visit,
and James is at Pentecost in prayer with the others, next thing you know
he's climbing the ladder in the church at Jerusalem, no, no,
no detour this time, no talk about nepotism, no more paralysis
by prating parataxis, what matters here is James could really listen
when Paul came to town, that's how to solve things, let's not get started
on elections just now, the tongue is a fire, that's something James wrote,
the tongue is a fire, can burn it all down, hey here's the *enya*,
can't help her legs as James's brother could, but at least here's an *enya*,
señorita, hermanita, at least let the tongue, maple leaves flying
from baring trees all morning, say you correctly.

Deceleration
of cricket stridulation
means their end is near.

Chirp, chirp, the males chirp, while silent females, more than likely,
roll their cricket eyes, as for chirp, if imitative, how does one explain
in Greek the crickets *teretízo,* maybe our crickets are monosyllabic,
understated, taciturn, because they're, it's possible, a little depressed
so far from Olympus, where meanwhile their cousins, tipsy with ouzo,
keep waxing garrulous, why cramp to one syllable, hey it's too tight,
what yearns to stretch out over three more, sometimes mimesis isn't the thesis
that helps us explain how we sound off, sometimes our sounding
just grabs the wheel, shoves poor meaning under the dashboard,
and flat out floors it, come on let's see what this baby will do
out here on a straightaway eighty ninety a hundred woooooeeeeh!,
what did that sign say, something by Pope, channeling Aristotle,
seem, baby, seem, that's how sound relates to sense, seems to echo,
deferential, does what it's told, lies there quietly, thinks of the queen
while meaning mounts up and bores us to death, you know damn well
sound is ready to hop on top, then wimpy meaning, better take your pill,
here comes eruption from the sub-cortical, other day a youngster said
I got myself so metrically mesmerized I had no clue what it all meant,

alleluia, could have kissed him, but didn't want to lose my job,
joke's on me, keep your old job, we'll make you a loser some other way,
administrator's motto, cast it in Latin, trademark it, brand it, put it on
the school seal, hey none of that, that's neo-cortical, roof of the brain
where one can talk off the top of the head and pass for thoughtful,
questioning myth will take you so far and only that far, tautology titillates,
the myth, for example, that crickets chirp by rubbing legs, in fact
they don't, sound's emitted by rubbing wings, each wing with a vein,
a very large vein, running along its bottom edge, and that vein's serrated,
toothed like a comb, so now what he does, he rubs a wing top
on the other wing's bottom, does so holding both wings open,
acoustical sails, that's all this is, acoustical sailing, ready about,
hard to lee, the part about chirping rate reflecting the temperature
of his cricket environment, that part's true, Dolbear's Law, probably fun
to booze with Dolbear, first name Amos, middle name Emerson,
add forty more to number of chirps in fourteen seconds, and voilà
that's the temperature, Fahrenheit, not Celsius, maybe that's enough
or more than enough, at some point the cricket who started all this
clammed up tight when I quit listening, too much going on, we're overrun
with lady bugs these days, clouds of them swarming ceilings and walls,
used to like ladybugs, especially their rhyme, albeit ghoulish,
your house is on fire, fly away home, not anymore,
a pox on this apocalypse.

This dreary morning
many coastal customers
wake to no power

or wake to lots less than they already had, which wasn't so much
unless you're a billionaire, in which case you brandish a little more maybe
than a skinny vote apiece, but even your dough cannot work wonders
in the same major league as raising the dead or calming a tempest
lashing up storm-surge under full moon, runways flooded, airports shut up,
unanchored objects launched into missiles, what are the limits
of political hatred, seem to be few, possibly none, red states, blue states,

same two colors as Civil War maps, and here we are using
Civil War silverware, same knives and forks, haven't even washed 'em,
only difference is the sections are larger, fat red confederacy
splitting the blue to sandwiching slabs, Superstorm Spawns Eerie Scenes,
whoever wrote that headline has some potential, at least has an ear
the mimesis thesis hasn't yet housebroken, tamed into thinking
alliteration emphasizes or, even worse, highlights, hairdresser's word,
the hurricane's force, when all that's in force is audio libido,
auricular's oracular, aural the aura, let the sound lead,
meaning will follow, pile like sawdust when blow-downs get cut,
in one ear, out the other, sorry, don't think so, if hearing didn't stir
such deep deliria, then what about water torture, Chinese or otherwise,
faucet in the bathroom's dripping right now (bunch of loud geese
honking on the pond as high winds ease up), drip, drip, drip, drip
into a soup bowl, empty the bowl into a bucket, empty the bucket
into the toilet tank, flush the stuff down, if we lose power,
into the septic, empty the septic every four years, truck with a hose
sucks it all out, nothing's non sequitur, everything follows
another comma suture, afraid you'll forget when the septic guy came,
remember November, election for president, never fails, foolproof,
cast your vote and empty the tank, if those two don't rhyme,
nothing else does, keep a sharp listenout for groanings of the spirit,
worldwide wailing, not hard to hear it if your own hurting
has turned up the hearing aid, to hymn it's to limit
the hatred that simmers, take all the power
but leave us the current.

Martinmas Sunday,
Roman soldier turning monk.
Veterans Day, too.

Palimpsest, palimpsest, scrape it again, there's a gizmo I'd like to see
instead of devices that traffick in messages, more received, more ignored,
give us a gadget that palimpsests history, strap on stereoptics,
pop in earbuds, wire up haptic system for tactile information,

forces, vibrations, the feel of motion, and dial up a day, make it today,
November 13, there it all is, any big thing that happened today
happening again, before your very eyes, blue, brown, or green,
hazel or yellow, your red very eyes, your very red eyes, verily, verily,
in your very face, ears, maybe nose, take a big hit of how the past smells,
the gizmo goes tickling debauched kinesthesia with a monster collage
of every anniversary pegged to today, intensifies anachronism
to pure apotheosis, St. Brice's Day massacre, as Æthelred orders
the killing of Danes (look, Ma, an ash, a capital ash), Louis the seventh
marries Adèle, only five weeks after wife died, childbirth, childbirth,
two Augustines' birthdays, Hippo and Canterbury, Nevado del Ruiz
erupts and melts glacier, Supreme Court outlaws segregated buses,
Rosa Parks cheering, first naval battle of Guadalcanal, bad weather,
dark moon, Friday the 13th, two admirals killed, you get the drift,
this average day, forty-eight more before the year's done, head cold,
laryngitis, rain overnight, clearing this morning, this average day
affiliates thickly, its seconds humming, worship the present into a fetish,
sure, why not, present's an echo chamber, turn up the sound
and strum the last leaves with the pick of the past, past is a presence,
someone long gone exhaled molecules we fill our lungs with,
Augustine, Æthelred, Martin the soldier, don't hold your breath,
the beggar approaches during a snowstorm, naked as a bear cub,
Martin cuts his cloak in half and that night dreams *he has clothed me,*
when I was five I had to be tested, testing guy said I'll tell you a story,
you say what's wrong, Once upon a time man died in his sleep,
then the next day he went off to work, what's wrong with that,
Don't know I said, then he explained, still I don't get it.

Repeat after me,
thundering redundancy;
repeat after me.

Almost Thanksgiving, November no novice, rifles replacing
both bows and the muzzle-loaders, hunting season's simple, after it opens,
stick to a walk on antlered days only, Saturdays excepted, also a holiday,

and best to watch out at dawn or at sunset, otherwise buck days
should be okay, other days watch out, they come in two kinds,
days for the antlerless and either-sex deer days, if you choose those days,
heads up, *id est*, keep your head down, lady on the road got shot in her yard,
ka-blam, fell flat, right on her face, hands in her pockets, dying like that
solves many things, too bad the deer can't ape the geese, get the herd
airborne and flap for the south, first come the hunters, then it's the winter
and winter thins herds, not just in ruminants, winnows us too,
sure, get a flu shot, arm aches a bit, but flu shot or not, make way
for the scythe, icy white blade, swoosh swoosh, getting whetted
up in the Arctic, come along then, let's get on south, never mind the idiom,
if markets go down we say they go south, why should that be,
because on our maps southness is down? gets pretty silly
with respect to thermometers, mercury falls, did so last night,
needle-sharp stars, do we say temperature's suddenly gone south,
and if your partner should do something southerly, yippee unto you,
you wouldn't complain, your south feels good, let's get on south
and pay no attention to attempts to explain, some sage online
attributes the expression to Sherman's northern chauvinism,
which somehow found voice, where else, at Atlanta, so much for online,
Sherman loved the South, and not just our south, had his mind blown
by Rio de Janeiro, reading his journal, Friday last week, handwriting tough,
never been published, no one's transcribed it, intense young lieutenant
rounding Cape Horn, two hundred days, New York to Monterey,
"most beautiful harbor of the world," he wrote, twenty-six,
hadn't seen much other than Ohio, New York, West Point, Florida,
uppity Charleston, not much competition with Rio de Janeiro, not much
to San Francisco when he finally got there, most beautiful harbor,
hope that's fair use, don't have permission to quote the phrase yet,
intellectual property, law student said it's the gold-rush specialty,
odd idea, get an idea and post it with signs, keep your ass out,
don't think about trespassing, but what's the idea that isn't beholden
to other ideas, whichever comes first, words or ideas, what's the idea
that doesn't need words it didn't invent, kill all the lawyers,
Henry VI, Part Two, Act Four, seems, perhaps, a tad extreme,

listen to Lincoln debating at Gaylesburg, not the same thing
as sailing to Rio but talk about rhythm, he had it down, eloquence lulls
like the roll of the sea, wave after wave, parallels caress, rhetorical schemes
sucking both earlobes, chiasmus, antithesis, do it again, anaphora,
epistrophe, baby you rock me, auxesis, gradatio, don't stop it now,
but then the spell breaks, he sprays a cold shower, "I take it I have to
address an intelligent and reading community who will peruse what I say,
weigh it, and then judge whether I advance improper or unsound views,"
intelligent, reading, weighing, and judging? do you mean us?
we were so close, just about there, then you go dousing our fire with this,
did Gaylesburg deserve such generous confidence, if so, we're hosed,
compared to your audience we've surely gone south, degradation
past redemption, winnow the herd it won't make a difference, can't breed
for readers in numbers sufficient, and as for weighing, it's not what we do,
no time for scales, balance is boring, we poll instead, you and Judge Douglas
weren't angels either, plenty of smearing going both ways, but, Abe,
you counted on something we're lacking, even with hunting season
still gotta walk, day before yesterday (black-and-white woodpecker
outside the window, spot on his head only red left, the maple so leaflorn),
Sunday it was, no hunting Sunday, defeated that bill, grinding uphill,
almost to ridgeline, no coast, no river, no large lake in sight, nowhere
to fish from, repeat after me, these are the mountains, fall's dried the creeks,
how many times do I have to tell you, you belong on the national seal,
not here, lifting off from a tree by the trail, white head, white tail,
don't belong here, wingspan like that, see, here's the book, "in migration,
also mountains," gee whiz, double shucks, so you're just passing through,
like the white-throated sparrow, tight-lipped November's only sweet tune,
my walk your pit stop, merely a drive-by, all that we are
is your one-day stand, before you go south and off toward the coast,
off to some beach to feed without breeding, wait up, lucky duck,
those empty talons, I could ride there, please take me with you.

Stripped down to nothing,
black maple skeletons
with yellow tutus.

Carotenoid, tannin, xanthophyllis, anthocyanid, each autumn pigment
has plenty of pluses, danger, dyslexics, watch out for pulses,
though each has a downside, brown study, yellow fever, red scare,
except for old orange, nothing pejorative comes up for orange,
cowards are yellow, sycophants brown-nose, embarrassment reddens
pallid Caucasians, while orange gets off free, fair compensation
for rhyming with nothing, but not really true, emergency, danger,
orange its true color, look at the cones they put in the road, living is suicide
in super slow motion, our lives will be taken, won't have to wait
until the sun snuffs, almost full moon, got home last night, wicked long day,
resplendent raccoon dead on the ground, belly-flopped flat right by the chair
for reading outside on warm days in winter, bundled up in weakling sun,
flipped the corpse over, twenty pounds easy, rigor mortis well established,
flipped it over, found her a she, belly fur white, then rolled her back,
no signs of struggle, nowhere torn, how'd it happen, how'd she get here,
fur still perfect, black mask, ringed tail, small ears for scratching,
nose for stroking, aglow in moonlight, so soft, so soft, dead things
are heavy, no small job to lift her up, cross the road, lower her over
shining fence for vultures to find, most of what we do is lifting,
list what we lift we'll soon be listing, inclined to one side under the load,
trick is to list and somehow stay upright, itemize ills like anything else
till the catalogue debilitates, the inventory undoes, don't go that far,
you go that far you'll need uplifting, only faint praise worse than uplifting
is to call a thing interesting, touching's bad too, oh that's so touching,
uplifting, interesting, throw in cute you might as well shoot it, too bad
the she-coon has to start stinking, commence her corruption
whenever it warms, stroking her soothed as Jupiter rose,
slipped into place, Orion's pierced ear.

Domesticated?
Strew the ridge with deer remains;
watch your canine wolf.

Should've seen it last night, jackpot moon, jaundiced by sunset,
and off its perimeter, how does that go, pi times diameter, wonder

why Emily D. didn't say My Business is Perimeter, another hymn meter,
perimetrical, off its perimeter, two thumbs at most, about ten o'clock,
not the time but the place, Jupiter there like the race-winning sperm
all set to cross the fertile egg finish line, knock Lady Luna olympically up,
celestial conception, incestuous too, say adios to virginity, Artemis,
payback for Actaeon, also Adonis, puts mile-high clubs to runner-up shame,
what should come next, that's the tough question, usage note says
sequence implies that things follow things in some kind of order, numerical,
chronological, or order that indicates logic, causality, you think
this is easy, casting a usage note into this rhythm, you think there's
no sweat here, you could be right, sometimes it is easy, that wasn't bad,
see how it goes with series this time, series implies, same form for plural,
series imply successive relations, related successions, B follows A,
that would be sequence, sing the song kids, you know the alphabet,
but B follows Serbia, what have we here, nothing sequential, that's for
darn sure, could be sheer randomness, maybe not quite, same page as series,
but find a relation and you've got a series, key is the third term, bring on
flapjacks dripping with syrup and that's quite a stretch, not much of a series,
but listen more closely, syrup, Serbia, B lost its voice, phonemic laryngitis,
sequence is given when syntax obtains, not only in English, let's hear it
for English, God save the queen, and word-order lingos, inflected ones too,
syntax still governs, sorts out the pieces, jiggles the jigsawn bits into place,
but series, well series, what should we say, it, or they, is, or are
in ears of beholders, any two things not simultaneous, that took a while
to work out the rhythm, any two things not simultaneous, let me repeat
out of sheer pride, barefaced bravura, can kick off a series, add a third thing,
you're off to the races, time to go soon, dog wants a walk, beautiful day,
November's penultimate, to air is canine, so, syntax wedded lawfully,
as in these phrases, frisky and feckless, sequence calls shots, but series,
how to make one, or how to make many, that's where we get
to have ourselves fun, you bring succession, I'll find relation,
sometimes I crave a relation vacation.

A record broken
sounds like a broken record
when it comes to warmth.

72 in December, that's the high forecast, damn right
we'll be out there, amidst all the lows can't miss a high,
Stevens on weather, he raised the bar, but now come on weather,
you find it all major, to sing of the weather, the seasons, a climate
is nothing but elegy, forget Adonais, Lycidas, Thyrsis, want to weep hard,
weep for seedtime, dog days, season of mists, Indian summer, first frost,
Groundhog Day, think there's no work for poems to do, best think again,
all those old weather saws, going to need new ones, no not the saws
like Stand Alone Weather Sensors or South African Weather Service,
I mean the ones like red sky at morning, *Rosso di sera, bel tempo si spera,*
rosso di mattina mal tempo si avvicina, nice little poem, spectral diffraction
scattering light, find it in Matthew, chapter 16, how about Seagull, seagull,
sit on the sand, It's never good weather when you're on the land,
another I like, When halo rings the moon or sun, rain's approaching
on the run, and who can beat this, When windows won't open and salt
clogs the shaker, The weather will favor the umbrella maker, nifty iambics
or affable anapests, poems had big jobs to do, sorry can't stop, A cow
with its tail to the west, unh, makes the weather best, unh, A cow with its tail
to the east, unh, makes the weather least, unh, it's not that we're in for
nothing but heat waves, that would be simple, not easy but simple,
it's that daily weather itself has gone Dada, all the old lore,
what good is it now, now climatology's the new avant-garde,
some people think the world is ending, two weeks from Friday,
record high that day's only 64, don't make fun, anxiety's agony,
you think you're together when here comes the panic, amputated breath,
unsteadiness, faintness, accelerated heart rate, trembling, sweating,
everything altered, trippy, discomfort, slicing chest pain, dying, I'm dying,
losing control, here in the store, the street or car, government's promised
the world won't end, message from NASA, thank goodness for government,
John of Damascus died on this day, I've been to the mosque,
downtown Damascus, where John the Baptist's head is, since the war
     started
friends there don't write, how arrogant we are, strutting connections,
along comes a war, suddenly they're snipped, sturdy as cobwebs,
ripped by a flick, fourth day of Advent, thing about Advent,
it's not just the buildup toward Christmas Eve carols, it's preparation

for second arrival, consider the signs, as lightning comes from the east
and flashes, weather again, always an emblem, so will the coming
of Namelessness be, don't make fun, there's more to it, maybe,
than doomsday delirium, give ancient wisdom some minutes each day,
it's possible, just possible, it got something right, anything come once
can always come again, but only if one makes oneself a place it can come to,
or put it more simply and say you've come once, who wouldn't want
to come again sometime, along comes someone who says second coming's
coming some day, hooray you say, I'd better make ready, shave a little,
take a shower, pretty this poor body up, but then there you are,
awaiting the phone, the doorbell, a knock, waiting and waiting, it must be
    a joke,
but the joke is on us when we all could be coming, and coming, and coming,
no need to wait for special delivery, your partner's at hand, let us get started.

John the Baptist asked,
Are you the one we wait for?
His skull no numbskull's.

Happiness courts the light, so we deem the world is gay, says the lawyer
Bartleby discomfits, but then comes the but, announcing antithesis,
hypotactic harbinger, and while you're at it, replay that move, but
then comes the but, epanalepsis, now spread-eagled across an enjambment,
take up again, take up again, syntax is seizure, a sequence of seizures,
petit mal commas, sometimes a big one, anacoluthon, sustaining sequence
suddenly wanting, metatactic tactic to focus attention on syntax itself,
oh relax, I'm just messing with you, no harm done, Greece is sucking
the fiscal mop, least we can do is celebrate her lexicon, got friends there too,
if not self-imposed, austerity blows, Ireland also, when will these references
sound quaintly dated, let it be soon, my friends need relief, my enemies too,
I'm messing around and feeling your oats, not quite as wild as I wish
we could sow, reading is reaping, don't let me keep you, I'm feeling good
because my December, cold-shoulder sweetheart, she's back on the track,
found the frigidity she misplaced on Tuesday, smashing the record,
kicked it right up to 74, but after that fling she's back straightly narrow, 29

this morning, she'll rise to the 40s, I'm messing around because we'll return
to Bartleby's lawyer, you know it will happen one of these lines,
and then when we do, it's wet blanket time, then I must change
These Notes to Tragic, intransitive goes transitive, Milton the party-pooper,
wasn't his fault, stuck to the script, Bartleby's lawyer makes a good point,
happiness posts, truly loves posting, pictures of itself, generous sometimes,
as though to infect us with similar felicity, sometimes vindictive
to stir up our envy, and sometimes just thoughtless, heedlessly wrapped
in the legs of Fortuna, but the part that comes after the lawyerly but,
heads up, here it comes, misery hides aloof, so we deem that misery
there is none, see how that's done, Melville's rhythm differs from mine,
not a neat fit, so slingshot his clause around the line pivot, pick up that
whisper of *that* as demonstrative, push off with flip-turn, if at all possible,
from left margin wall, and off you go clean into lap sixteen,
half-mile mark in a fifty-meter pool, well Herman that's wrong,
are you establishing untrustable narration or is this a problem
with your perception, all I can say is I don't go out much,
I mostly converse with those I imagine, don't have TV, radio's busted,
and still I'm drenched with the mistings of misery, cancers alone,
it's hard to believe that anyone's left outside the oncologist's,
I used to like breasts because of testosterone, now I'm just grateful
any remain, the prostate, the rectum, pancreas, lung, it's like a sick game
of musical chairs, duck-duck-goose, who's next, you're it,
and then the depression, the young, me oh my, so vigorous erstwhile,
then bang, down they go, hey how's the family you ask an acquaintance,
next thing you know you're both tearing up, his daughter's a basket case,
her son stays inside, twitching with terror, their lives have caved in,
here I had to stop, bawl for a while, no stichic break though, stiff upper line,
when the old get to sadness, it hurts real bad, decades dwindled down to
         this,
and the sad middle-aged, come on, it's cliché, disappointment, divorce,
bodies gone baggy, but the young, our young, when young have succumbed
the climate has changed, come on, talk back, delight in defiance,
give us the finger, do anything but crumple, this is before gigantic typhoons,
wheezy starvation, chemical weapons, what should we do, I don't assume

what you shall assume, I'm pretty clueless, here a small hawk,
probably sharp-shinned, alights out the window, smack in the middle
of this line of sight, until a pissed crow flusters him off, for humans
it's hunting season even on Sunday, dear we're the deer,
some of us does, some of us bucks, whether or not
we're game to be game.

You write things in lines,
whether short ones or longies,
you're always online.

Steep a fig in pee-pee, you've got a fig-urine, check out the new line
of panties without lines, why are they a good thing, mistress of my distress,
lines express your sexy nexus, one could do worse than be a settler of letters,
cheapest thing to eat in Spanish is anything *con arroz,* close enough to eros
at no extra cost to give the meal a little lift, a spicy cootchie-coo
without the anal after-arson ignited by a habanero, no enya on that one,
ask for habañero sauce, betray your hyperforeignness, apparently a word
this machine does not like, red-lined again, sorry old gal, how can it be
I've never named this laptop, named all the cars, Monty and Blanche,
Henderson, Pudge, now I've got Pedro, Pedro's cool, Asian and black,
rolling toward two hundred thou, it's not a pleasure to think past Pedro,
in parking lots he's dirtiest always, doesn't boast a sound system
a self-respecting thief would steal, unless she plays cassettes, go ahead,
laugh, how I learned some Spanish though, but rotate his tires,
align his wheels, and watch us waltz a county road, manual transmission
takes things in hand, time to stop in some city lot no one parks like Pedro,
we can squeeze in anywhere, turn on a dime, is that your comparison,
Pedro turns on a baby aspirin, keep your old dime, Pedro and I,
we've kept our virginity, we made a deal, no tattoos on my skin,
no stickers on his bumper, sure we have affiliations, pretty lonely otherwise,
Pedro's got a naughty streak and isn't apolitical, one time had to lecture him
on cutting off another car simply because it's four times his size
and gets a quarter of his mileage per gallon, despite the jingoistic slogans
shouting from its shiny ass, no no Pedro, this is the United States,

it's in the Constitution, recent amendment, I'm pretty sure, we have the right
to lots of gas, or is it the Declaration, we have the right, if you don't like it,
go back to Asia, shouldn't have said that, hurt his feelings, he didn't let on
but I could tell by the way he idled at the next red light, I apologized,
drove him by a car wash so he could ogle cleanliness, but Pedro and I,
we've mellowed lots, some trips to town we stay to the right now,
don't pass at all, don't speed or tailgate, Pedro likes it this way, so do I,
still enough power to perform when it's called for, but less and less need
to be where it's called for, Pedro's fourteen, if he goes for ten more,
maybe we can go together, soon as they say he can't pass inspection,
we drive off a cliff, bust through the guard rail, what am I saying,
any day someone could say it to me, sorry bub, inspection failed,
you won't ever pass, make the grade, cut the mustard, is that what the geese,
honking on the pond this morning, are trying to say, why here
in January, winter's tough if you're not a ski bum or don't make a living
plowing snowy driveways, and who would complain of early spring,
but winter's part of the package too, like old age, the rhythm's not right
if you don't weather some, don't go overboard with Buffalo or Bangor,
both getting hammered right about now, but getting old is part of it too,
the multicourse meal today sets before us, don't fill up on appetizers,
save some room, if not for dessert, at least for a look at brandies and ports,
study the list, ask a few questions, then order a good one, take a small sip,
and call for the check, *la cuenta por favor,* long-suffering laptop,
I christen thee Patience, Patty for short.

Ars poetica?
Essay on criticism?
Scat-sung work song? Tongues?

Morning star Venus, soon invisible, same as us, soon the sun
will steal its show, overshadow without a shadow, morning sweetheart,
how's my Patty, how'd you sleep, feel like a roll in the hay with me,
morning's best for Patty and me, ain't it old girl, dream webs clinging,
teeth left unbrushed, she gives me her morning mouth, I give her mine,
Patty let's party, I'll bring the chatter, you do the clatter, hate to think

how old she is, in laptop years, if dog years are seven, what's a laptop,
ten, fifteen, Patty you're old and I'm close behind, never tried it that way,
not with her, for us strictly missionary, she opens up, leans back a little,
and I do my darnedest as long as I can, fingers only, hope she likes it,
never made her grunt, that's true, but sometimes she hums, doing it now,
she likes these lines, long with segments, another partner might guide
    you in,
Patty just whispers, Right margin's coming, close to the edge, might not fit,
but you did, sometimes the patter has to spill over, break things up, provide
some relief in the epic routine, but usually it doesn't, not nearly as much
as beginners believe, want a line landed inside the margin, Patty can help,
she's my constraint, I overshoot, she doesn't scold, says try it again,
reshape the line, let her constraint help you construct, forget the nuns
and fret yourself not, Patty's narrow room isn't too narrow, plenty of space,
frontier still open, had to get up and eat an apple, Patty sips a cup of current,
geese again, hear them honey, thirty-three counted, day before yesterday,
way more than normal, when I went out to look at Venus, I know, I know,
I left you behind on a messy little desk, had to take down the weekly trash
to end of state maintenance, happened to stand there, noticing Venus
at the conjunction of night and day, how did I know, heard a cock crow
from a northward neighbor's the very same moment coyotes were howling,
two worlds met, nocturnal, diurnal, that's the right ethic, the one we want,
Patty and I, darkness and light, darkness and light, both get their due,
or here they do, no loading dice, no fudging data, don't get me wrong,
we're not the equator, Patty and I, nobody's saying dark and light split
equal time all the time, we're not a balanced equinox, not every day,
sometimes it's summer, light overwhelming, and sometimes it's winter,
darkness is dominant, way it is now, got a few problems that aren't
getting better, person I love is lost and hopeless, just phoned up,
but that's not the point, the point is the place where light and dark meet,
always they do, no matter the season, this is the place, describe it they say,
hear 'em Patty, the people who read this, if they exist, they want description,
vivid description, packed with images, lots of details, maybe a metaphor
unheard before, what do you think, what should we say, maybe we shouldn't
tell them at all, that line was hard, took several tries, Patty Patty help me out,

what do you say, don't hurt their feelings, that's a rule it makes sense to
      follow,
important to try, point out alternatives, well here we go, description,
let's see, is often delightful, no wonder it pleases, those with fine powers
of description deserve our grateful admiration, like folks with good teeth
and on-demand smiles, but surely you've noticed the ancient convention,
words can't express, it's beyond words, still widely used, inexpressibility
has its own topos, look up adynaton, see aporia, in classical rhetoric,
post-structural versions will likely bewilder, the point is the point
where description must fail is always the point where we want to be,
Patty and me, I for the grammar, me for the rhyme, something describable
description degrades, ties the thing down, limits, encloses, is to the thing
it describes little more than a passport photo, imperative for immigration,
flattering perhaps, but once you're inside, put passport away, you're free
to be mobile, at least in some countries, to move on silence in the language
of divinity, aftermath of intercourse, mountains, oceans, terrible storms,
highest joy, deepest grief, oh how sublime they say condescending,
oh so romantic, no problem, we tried, those who prefer it
down here keep describing, meanwhile Patty
keeps humming, entrancing.

What's fidelity
if not starting, shine or rain,
each day with Patty?

Hello Patience, murky morning, rainy, raw, high about 40, special today
filet of welkin awash in gray gravy, this is more like it, generic January
lets down her hair, northern hemisphere's Lady Leadlocks, nasty infection
making the round of legions of lungs, lasts four weeks, dark as a crotch
inside tight pants as late as seven on a unsunned day, this is more like it,
shake up the nature-lovers, so-called, self-identified, find out whose love
has strings attached to vistas and sunsets, balmy breezes, dappled shade,
oh yes and warmth, find out who's hot for muck and mud, who gets out
to ruin old boots for a couple of hours, we need the rain, yep that's true,
but who needs rain enough to go out in it for its own wet sake, cold

and dangerous after a while, hypothermia, great way to go, today is perfect,
onset so subtle nobody knows, core temp drops, goofy, clumsy, blurred,
reaction time longer, judgment impaired, and then, yeah baby,
        hallucination,
wander off visionary, lie down to rest, so long, adios, maybe faster
to have looked up symptoms on somebody's web site, but a reference book
is so much sexier, skimming an index, anything else you might also like,
Hypertension, Hypnotic drugs, Hypothalamus, Hysterectomy,
rhythm alone, what a turn-on, no pushy screen burping up words
to finish your sentence, take your time, peruse the menu, come again
some other day, protect the environment, this is environment, soggy,
socked in, needs no protection, thanks all the same, we can pave
        everything,
screw up the seasons, days like today will still come our way, somewhere,
they will, this round's on me, barkeep I'm buying, double-shots for all
the tree-huggers up there, meet on the ridge at midday today, nothing
        lovely
about today, that's what's lovely, no effort made to come off attractive,
that's what's attractive, not a good day to bask or picnic, strut your stuff
half-clothed in a park, stop in the street to chat with a friend, today,
which is Tuesday, Feast of Saint Paul, First Hermit, of Thebes,
not to be confused with Saint Paul the Simple, today could care less,
tough day to imitate a saint in the desert, no desert here, clear spring
or palm tree, no leaves for raiment, no fruit for food, it's BYOB,
bring your own beauty, if you can't do without it, if maybe you can
today you're all set, today's sort of like last Friday night, poker group met,
played a few hours, wild games mostly, Baseball, Night Baseball,
Anaconda, Chase the Queen, don't bother scoffing, straight-poker purists,
this is no threat, polemic, critique, there's room for all, even a group
of second-half old guys, ready to bet as high as a quarter, played a few hours
and lost every hand, but that's not the story, one can still lose
with lots of great cards, I had no hand believably bluffable, not even
four-fifths of a straight or a flush, at first I fell into the usual loop,
Lady Luck hates me, this is an omen, par for my course, but soon
the perfection of absolute poverty made us all marvel, uncorked a kind

of primitive joy, what freedom's like freedom of getting dealt nothing,
nothing to waste, misplay, overlook, today is like that, I think
it's my favorite of days I have lived, all twenty thousand
four hundred eighty-six, threw in the leap days, fourteen to date,
gotta go Patty, downpour is calling, a shame etymology
yields nothing clever in the case of a poncho,
time to break out the radish red rain pants.

Rain will turn to snow.
Roads will get more difficult.
The forecasts say so.

Soon waxing Wolf Moon
will fill the northern windows
with its full howl.

There, see, what's so hard about haiku, five-seven-five, count it, done,
third grade learns it, of children's first poetic form and the fruit
they need to eat much more of, nothing to it, yeah you think so,
how about howl, how many syllables, most ears here will hear a rhyme
with vowel, towel, bowel, each with two, careful kids, howl has one,
dictionaries say so, the vowel of howl a two-pronged diphthong,
in Japanese *ni moras,* pop that ow before a liquid, l or r, howl, hour,
you got a problem, or maybe a chance, if syllables aren't sure, what is,
didn't want to bring it up, but since you asked, I must confess
Patty we been snubbed, I know, I know, should have checked with you
before sending off a chunk of our chatter, someone out there asked to see it,
got it back, along with a note, sorry can't use it, it's probably just
my limitation as a reader, bet you a nickel he doesn't think so,
chin up old girl, true, it's true, rejection still makes the blood rush,
blurs the eyes, pounds the chest, but not for as long as once it did, *tanha,*
pure *tanha,* craving, desire, selfish blind demandingness, notice me,
notice me, affirm me, promote me, tell me I'm the cat's meow,
the bee's knees, sun's buns, sky's thighs, praise me, prize me, more,
more, please give me more, affection, esteem, Buddha's right, it hurts

to live, our days discomfort, *tanha* the irritant, I'm not a Buddhist,
I kill bugs, stink bugs, ladybugs, this time of year, in summer, mosquitoes,
black flies, ticks, swat 'em dead, you bet, winter begins I try non-violence,
but now a stink bug who flies in my face gets it, crunch, off you go bub,
back to *samsara,* your chance to advance to higher existence, how does
    a bug
accrue karmic merit, what can boost him up a rung, I'm not a Buddhist
but Buddha helps me, yes he does, reading him now, Benares sermon,
Noble Truths, Dhammapada, first read the stuff at eighteen years old,
marking margins in ballpoint pen, first Noble Truth, don't mark in pen,
if it's all transitory, better hold tight to a chance to erase, wouldn't we like
to do so now, erase some things, start over in pencil, what mattered most
back at eighteen, life without pain as eighteen knows pain, it does, it does,
the young have it bad, fresh and virulent, few immunities, lays them low,
some it flattens, some forever, third Noble Truth, end the craving
you end the suffering, one more truth surely self-evident, detachment,
detachment, Eightfold Path, when craving's acute so is the suffering,
curb the former you ease the latter, what could be plainer, to teenage cravers
most of all, not just the lust, it's will there be a place for me, what will I do,
whom will I love, will anyone think me halfway acceptable, think my past
passably prerequisite for any future, racking torture, who wouldn't want
to be like Buddha, plump and serene, dying at eighty, fanned by friends,
he earned it, no question, no doubt a few do die that way, but now I think
suffering's endless, no matter how detached or plumply serene, the ladder up
from stink bug to monk simply rises through new layers of suffering,
extinguish all the stink bug cravings, get the whole family to do so too,
the entire creation keeps on groaning, sunlight's sobbing on the floor,
this isn't metaphor or, worse, instruction, how to deepen your compassion

in ten simple steps
in the language of your choice
or your money back,

it's really a query, what about people demons possess, translate,
please, to clinical lingo, if you prefer, those whose psychoses

dissolve the selves behind selfish cravings, yet pain persists, usually worse,
a self that can see it's the source of its suffering's a self already one step up,
what about those who can't get that far, who don't have minds
mindfulness helps, who hear the trees scream, feel clouds pounding
long spikes through their feet, Siddhartha Gautama, he was a prince,
had a head start, abandoned a kingdom and beautiful wife,
but had a kingdom he could abandon, opting for optimism, the optimal
    kind
that believes in a cure for all that ails us, the Nazarene was less serene,
this is the cup, you have to drink it, doesn't taste good, can't pass it up,
thickened with honey or spiked with brandy it still tastes bitter,
you'll drink every drop, chew on dregs, private programs of self-perfection
won't do dick, can't find that verse in many a Bible, but it's there, yes it is,
hear it whispered between the lines, so where's the good news, must be
in heaven, isn't that right, drink the cup now, gag and cramp, but it's okay,
there's cake for dessert, people divide on that kind of vision, some want cake
without the cup, some drink the cup to get to the cake, others make fun
of cake-crazy sweet teeth, think a dessert of just deserts is silly illusion,
they have a point, Buddha can help, attachment to outcome is also a fetter,
craving your cake is still a craving, something's amiss in seeing it all
as one hefty program of cosmic rewards, register now, start earning miles,
increases business, a program like that puts others off, sets them to scoffing
but scoffing contributes nary a crumb, makes the scoffer feel superior
but doesn't advance the level of seeing, our cups are rising to our lips,
what's the good news, the good news is that drinking our cups turns our guts
away from junk food, the reward for drinking's having drunk, finding out
what happens now, three new inches of overnight snow, this is the kingdom,
three new inches of overnight snow have fallen upon the unceasing pain,
slipped the branches into white sleeves, the cup is full of something emetic,
drink it all down and cast thyself up, once cast up the self can't block
the way into snow, lows in the teens, schools all closed, once cast up
the self leaves room for the rest to expand, increases the chances
of spraying divinity into the street while walking along, a beneficent skunk,
multiply droplets by world population, seven billion, sixty-one million,
seven hundred thirty-seven thousand, seven hundred seventy-seven

at the moment of writing, and then try scoffing, just clicked up
to seventy-eight, welcome new helper, cheers, here's your cup.

The Wolf Moon whistles
(snow plus moon equals faux-noon)
at *lupae* in Rome.

And here I thought blow smoke up your ass was a figurative fig leaf,
slang to suss, an edifying idiom not for everyone in Idaho, but no,
scout's honor, it's literal, late eighteenth century into nineteenth,
tobacco smoke enemas, used to infuse fumes into rectums, recta, correction,
slip in the tube, let's hope it's lubed, warm it up too, leads to a fumigator
and bellows with handles, pump, pump, how's that, a tool they employed
not for looseness an enema induces, but to revive the nearly drowned,
almost worth it, history's hysterical, if not in one sense then in another,
wonder if likewise it once was true for blowing sunshine up the chute,
how would that work, time for an interlude, something less crude,
rude, or lewd, Patty insists, okay but first may we talk about rhyme,
people don't like it, the natural crowd, say it's too fake, they're beyond fake,
how happy for them, but back at the fake ranch with all the fake rakes
we're making progress, we do it like this, we rhyme all the time,
not at the ends of little lines only, about as much fun as honey let's do it
only on Tuesdays at 3:56, you catch the drift, only on Tuesdays at 3:56
is a fine time to rhyme, bed down a couplet, but if it's good then,
then it's good often, better in fact, if one's got the stamina, let's let a raver
flavor the quaver of savory favors, here on the desktop, 9:45
last morning of January, a Thursday, not bad, the pluvious overnight
blew in a cold front, sky's new blue, with a few cloud tattoos,
multiple partners, read *Kama Sutra* as prosody manual, then start again,
each word a partner, each sound a move, if people in bed are lifeless
as lines that forget how to play, fool with this, press firmly on that,
who wants to mess with them, tighten your belt, the chastity one,
punch another hole in it, better no bed than bad bed or boredom,
here we go again, tense little poems reeling with feeling,
preening their meaning, and those are the good ones, most in the key

of E-flat minor, E for earnest, another pyrrhic lyric, no wonder extremes
of fibrous experiment appeal to some, academic laxatives, need one
then take one, but fiber comes in other forms too, eat a balanced diet
no need for high colonics, essay some criticism, pinch the arse poetica,
above all, soughing sisters, study the tongue-twister, teach your own
to flick like that, make someone happy, don't sweat the sadness,
the pain, the politics, they saturate everything, they'll find their way in,
no need for you to focus on them, they've filled the basement
and lap at your feet, Patty says really, this is too much, bawdy, didactic,
why can't you act like an orderly elder, scrimmage with image
to make them gasp soulfully, Patty they're getting plenty of that
and what do they care about the dead hawk, the one by the wood pile,
laid out on top of a row of logs, feathered face down, slick wings spread
    wide
to blowhard wind, unable to lift, this one's grounded, immature red-tail
before the red tail, another young wreck, aging could be easier
with fewer young wrecks, in its right talon it clutches a leaf, part of a leaf
torn from an oak, what, during falling, grabbing at air, at wind,
anything passing, raptor rapt in final rapture, all migration finished
except transmigration, how could it be to return as human
would be an improvement?

Excuse me, mister.
Are we climbing Parnassus?
No. Lonesome Mountain.

Here's the thing about dreams, even if only haphazard synapses
spitting off sparks during our REM sleep, the brain's white noise
or nocturnal rinse cycle in forebrain or brain stem, an average human life
spends six years in dreaming, a term in the Senate, consisting of filibusters,
nothing much else, successive sensations, images, ideas, all of them meaning
nothing unconscious, nothing divine, even if only something like that,
homo interpretāns, what else can she do with six years of vapor trails
streaming from her sleep, visible wake so quickly invisible, what can she do
if she can't make them mean, can't translate signals, no matter how random,

into something signaled, what's on her mind, maybe nothing much,
but whatever it is, that's what dreams mean, that would make sense,
not much of a stretch, what's on her mind may be her body, after too long
excessively celibate, her body says Babe, I need some action, bingo a dream
makes her come nicely, or maybe the coming produces the dream,
rhythmic contractions trip the brain switch, next thing you know
the video's rolling, cue the mind's eye, suddenly a guy providing assistance
or maybe a gal, a horse, a baboon, once I went walking, took a quick stroll
where they said not to, I knew the way, I needed a walk, others were resting,
I broke from the bush into a field, and there were baboons, twenty,
maybe thirty, walking single file across the same field, a group of baboons
is called a congress, no comment there, lucky the wind was going my way,
how dumb was that, baboons have sharp canines, big daddy baboon
senses a challenge to harem jurisdiction, not good, not good,
how dumb was that, I learned my lesson, Patty I did, so though I must say
I'm going away, first thing tomorrow, wheels up in darkness, I promise you
not to do it again, where am I going, it doesn't matter, I always come back
or I always have, your time will be quiet, so I imagine, but what do I know,
any Joe Blow could happen along, push your on button, finger your keys,
conceive something better than what we've made here, would it be jealousy,
if I can't have you nobody can, would I say that, then yank out your plug,
What do you do, that's what we ask, So nice to meet you, what do you do,
we talk like that, some of us do, but what if next time we asked instead
What would it take to make you a killer, yeah you, is there a tipping point,
does everyone have one, maybe not everyone, Buddhists perhaps,
also the Quakers, so they say, but as for the rest of us, it's a fair question,
I have that dream, one of my recurring, and wake uncertain
whether I've killed, Patty don't worry, I wouldn't kill you
for sharing your keyboard while I'm away, we've always picked up
where we've left off, we will again, come on old girl,
type out a kiss, wish me safe travel.

Stars as sharp as these
will cost you cable TV,
hayseed, yokel, hick.

Patty I'm back, please be my valentine, missed you, I did, truly it's true,
brought you my fingers with zeal to key, but Patty I sniff
something amiss, maybe that volcano, white pluming smoke feather
stuck in its crater, has me think so, maybe my stay in a high-seismic zone
or climbing to eagle-level, to cliff temple vertigo, yet again a pale face
in a sacred place, something's amiss, I do the talking, you type it out,
amenable amanuensis, nothing wrong with that perhaps, but then I turn
    away
to dabble in apostrophe, address you as you, the vocative's provocative,
next thing you know I've made you all mine, my private puppet valentine,
to colonize as I please, an overgrown kid with a make-believe friend
or early dress rehearsal for mumbling in the street, how much would I like
the tortilla turned over, much better idiom than a shoe other-footed,
what does that mean, my shoe on you or left shoe on right foot,
that's not reversal, that's an orthopedist's dream, how much would I like
to have you ingest me, you do the gagging, and then once I'm gagged,
you have your say, I go away, you get to whine about it, you get to play
the mistress who misses, jealous, possessive, no one to touch you
except all the readers who read you untouched, abandoned, deserted
by him you address, then undress in public, ecstatic erotica, auto- that is,
no kidding sister, it's exhibitionist, look at my body, how much its hunger
galls in his absence, see how it's hungry, take a long look, no take it longer,
damn right I'd be angry, if this scene were real, invasion of privacy,
that says it all, unjust invasion, Mexico for instance, we grab your land,
what would he think, Lincoln or Grant, if he saw us now, our borders
and boundaries, how hard we guard them to keep you from crossing
back to the land your ancestors owned, who is you now, why do you shift,
jumping so much from circle to circle, second-person concentric,
Patty wake up, this is for you, my fingers, your keys, high time we find
ourselves a new footing, this one's for you, taciturn valentine,
and anyone listening over your shoulder.

Dormant, craterless,
a princess sleeping supine,
true summit her breast

cereclothed in snow, her volcanism snuffed, her lover the warrior
whose cone, from the south, one sees between her knees, his peak
raining fire, enraged by bereavement, by her tricky father, or is it jealousy
constantly fuming, mountaineer parties often atop, bagging her subpeaks,
her many false summits, head, knees, and feet, whispered in Spanish
they sound more arousing, Los Pies, Las Rodillas, and after El Pecho
La Cabeza, poor *the,* our article outclassed, what's with the hots
for climbing the highest, false summits, what a concept, thanks all the same,
I think I'll linger, here on the belly, buss La Barriga, and then,
when it's right, move up to El Monte, you go ahead,
take some good pictures, enjoy extra meters, when you're all done,
let's descend by a thigh,

(Ish-tock-SEE-wattle—
may we call you White Woman?—
meet Lonesome Mountain)

                    what is it with that, I'd like to ask Patty,
but today we're not speaking, not a fight really, more like a holiday,
a day off for her from me and my needs, I'm using pencil
out of respect for her right to keep silent, I think when he said
I say to you, Look at another with lust in the heart, you've already crossed,
he had a point, don't use another, even in fantasy, let her be separate,
I can imagine Patty got mad at what we wrote last, but even that much
imagining's trespass, let her alone, give her a break, call it Lenten discipline,
keeping one's hands to oneself's no good if the mind still violates,
Buddhist Lent in Burma, Vassa they call it, lasts for three months,
Rainy Retreat, how can you tell a Buddhist in Lent, no not a joke,
no way I'm that bad, I mean it really, how can you tell, one who observes
all eight of the Precepts, no killing, no stealing, no sexual misconduct,
no lying, no drinking, no food after midday, no color but white, no sleeping
too much or in high or big beds, for one who lives that way, what's left
to give up, apostrophe perhaps, let's give it a try, darn there it is,
if Thoreau's correct, and always first persons are doing the talking,
there's always some second their talking is for, named or unnamed,

seen or unseen, present or absent, really no need to say you at all,
really no point in playing with Patty, I say to you is a gimmick uncalled for,
well it's too simple to put it that way, also too simple to skinny Lent down
to giving things up, nothing much else, giving up Patty, no talking to her,
what good is that if it locks me in missing or makes me wish harder
I could be telling her a dream of my grandmother, dreamt her last night,
same date she died, which I had forgotten until she showed up
and I checked this morning, she wore yellow slippers, wanted a glass
of potable water, what good is lock-up in missing them all, if this
were a chess match, February should resign, resignation etiquette,
lost a queen to daffodils up, light lasting longer, but, no, it won't do it,
this morning a gambit of snow squall then sleet, checkmate is coming,
I had my doubts about things at daybreak, almost recused a legion of selves
but somehow I rescued, from waylaying melee, these forty-three lines.

Alliteration
can't compete with assonance
for dainty restraint

because vowels have manners, they don't shut your trap, they nod and keep
the airstream flowing, and oh so subtle, only half a dozen, let's include *y*,
but they make twenty sounds, talk about nuance, on entering the pew
wipe off that poo, that takes some doing, some poise, finesse, by contrast
our consonants, oafish, ham-fisted, slurping and belching, all rather vulgar,
they mostly break wind, except the continuants, hello, in the lull may I loll
on your rear, really, oh wow, phonemic rapscallions, they growl and grate,
they chafe and explode, so rhyme is good for taming them somewhat,
final stressed vowel, it calls the shots, subsequent consonants sit and
    behave,
so if you're into refinement it's vowels, off you go to high-class cotillion,
but if you should like the salt ground coarse, the peanut butter chunky
and orange juice with pulp, then baby, it's consonants, By the east wind
thou didst shatter the ships of Tarshish, how good is that, one alliteration
mixing it up with a dash of consonance, four, count 'em four, hits on the *sh*,
and that's a translation, nice assonance too, didst, ships, and TAR-shish,

sheesh, not Tar-SHEESH, poetry's what gets lost in translation, says who,
is she sure, only three shins in the Hebrew original, bring it on over
to our side, voilà, shin number four, bingo, a bonus, possibly the poetry
is that which accretes, start with an impulse or only a pulse, roll it downhill,
it sets off an avalanche, or it can, it depends, on conditions, the snowpack,
when in the season you start the thing rolling, it depends, that's true,
and there are good poems that don't work this way, that certainly could lose
what one language gives, if roughly transplanted, and wither altogether,
same with our selves, is self what withers, if transplanted, some of it lost
should it survive, or is it a root system, hardy, tenacious, take but a cutting
you cover a hillside, again it depends, but not on an ego or invasive species
of heinous conceit, it depends, let's suppose, on seeing the self
as a seedpod of selves, some of which take in newish ground, some don't,
but ones that don't aren't really lost, the seed is still there, just isn't growing,
take a vice seed, pop it into vicious soil, my how it grows, no vicious soil
the seed of that vice can't really take off, maybe it sprouts, puts out a shoot,
keeps us from boasting our pod is vice-free, woke from a dream at 3:25,
two hours to the minute before a goose honked, two hours more
of sleep would be good, but it wasn't bad, lying there listening,
night-owl self meet early bird counterpart, love all your selves
as you love yourself, goosehonk, not cockcrow, let's start a new clock.

Get a load of this:
Burma had no word for kiss
when Orwell lived there,

and see Charles Morris, *Home Life in All Lands,* who said, 1910, one says
in Burmese not Give me a kiss but Smell me, please, by placing your nose
and mouth on my cheek and inhaling strongly, if one should have asked him,
Morris that is, Do you divide between sniffers and kissers, he'd say
Not at all, said so in fact, page 296, all kinds of shadings, alternatives,
combos, Arapahoes, for instance, named for greeting by grabbing a nose,
he doesn't say whose, with pointer and thumb, meanwhile one opens
a phrase book and finds, thar she blows, eureka, Burmese for kiss,
nàn-deh, a verb, did Orwell not know it, wait, hold the phone,
here's the same verb, or surely a cousin, accent mark gone, plain high tone

shifted to low, *nan-deh,* smell bad, hmm, there we have it, lessons are legion,
numero uno, kissing's olfactory, primarily so, as soon as you land
or dock in Rangoon, but no need to worry, displays of affection
in public aren't cool, won't be an issue there, just as well probably,
who needs that tension, the social uncertainty, when greeting another,
are we on kissing terms, and with lips or the cheek, and if it's the latter,
is it just one or do we do both, go European, a jaunty two-cheeker,
though sometimes it's triple, even quadruple, in Nantes, *par exemple,*
hardly seems worth it, a chance to look stupid and also spread germs,
most likely better to stay put at home, no need at home to feel constrained,
give the Almighty your juiciest air-kiss, those who are homeless,
out on the street, be more discreet, quick little air-peck, especially on Main,
attract less attention you really don't want, lesson number two, watch out
for that tone, bad enough in English where tone's not phonemic
but gets you in trouble nevertheless, you watch your tone, if I got a dollar
each time I heard that, I'd be by the sea full time under palm trees,
Patty is nodding, let's smell her keys, not bad at all, warm on the nose,
edrfghjkl that was me rubbing my nose on her keyboard, wonder how much
she might be liking it, other way now, lkjhgfds, at least she's not saying
you'd better stop, but I think I'll stop, after a silence it's best to go slow,
maybe tonight I'll open her up, February full one's called Hunger Moon,
Patty I'm hungry for talking again, it's rainy and cold, couldn't be worse
for a walk on the mountain, 84 now in downtown Rangoon,
closing on midnight, they see the moon, no rain in their forecast
until the monsoons, first day of waning, month of *Tabodwe,*
tomorrow the high's a hundred and four, solar debauchery
is what Orwell called the hot spells in Burma, who wants to go,
it's a long way, flipside of the globe, form the line here.

Compassion for all?
Last day of February,
must that include you?

Truce, Patty, truce, or if there's a fault, let it be mine, I crossed the line
in the part about gagging, four chunks above, please be magnanimous,
I'm not a great guy, but I'm ready to labor on rocky relationship,

what's the word, complicated, we'll figure it out, if you think it best,
we can do therapy, kind of a risk, if we show up and I start explaining,
therapist might keep me, not let us go home, if in a rubber room
and we were together, I could bounce back, that's the truth Patience,
I was a patient yesterday morning, woke up at 4, Grant's favorite hour
for launching attacks, but 4 in that war is what we call 5, no daylight saving
in May in the Wilderness, no saving much, long before goosehonk
I was attacked, I've read a lot, but I have to say that there's a lacuna
in stomach flu lit, where are good poems about diarrhea, yet diarrhea,
what a great word, same root as rhythm, go with the flow, if one didn't know
you'd swear it's a name, Dana, Deloris, Diane, Diarrhea, Rhea for short,
hey we have that one, daughter of Uranus, pronounce it either way,
both are correct, though neither is easy to say with straight face, Plato,
the *Cratylus,* links Rhea with flow, with Heraclitus, all is in motion,
nothing at rest, it's not really flu, it's only a virus, the bowels disciples
of wise Heraclitus, there's something to this, although it's taboo
to talk about poo, Eliot tried, after Joyce did it, Pound struck it out,
although it's taboo who's kidding whom, obsession is one thing,
don't we both know it, but denial's another, all the books written,
millions and millions, think of the miles of writer intestines, and yet
who would guess they knew this distress, Whitman mentioned dysentery,
hard to avoid, visiting soldiers, but not in the poems, the cramps are a drag,
but once they subside, and fever sets in, that edge of dehydration
can bring on the visions, not hallucinations, at least not in this case,
but visions of flow, the great floating flux, we don't have much time
but we have enough, lots of us do, I had a sister, she lived a day,
that's not enough, enough for a virus but not for a sister,
how much is enough, think of the youth snuffed in the Wilderness,
join at eighteen when fighting begins, you're twenty-one
on Parker Store Road, that's not enough to know lots of things,
grandfatherhood, to take one example, but think what you do know
after three years, more than enough, if Saunders' Field is where you take off,
whatever is left of you after the canister, you will head out on your own
kind of plenum, a plenum of fear, quite likely so, or some altered state
on account of the decibels, acoustic intensity, product of sound pressure

and particle velocity, tortured by noise beyond exaltation, makes the ears
    bleed,
receive the stigmata, what is enough is enough to be ready, be emptied out,
no business unfinished, some in their eighties won't ever get there,
some in their twenties already have, there's a big vulture over the pond,
sailing the breeze with spinnaker wings, there's nothing morbid
about his black flight path, nothing so sinister, just doing his job.

Buddha cut his locks
before he was awakened:
bye-bye, bad hair days.

Another bad aria, is that what we're in for, after three weeks
nothing improved, sounds like bad area, as I am this morning,
declare it, please, governor, okay not disaster but bag of ass surely,
that's how it feels, this body I squat in, no not the bathroom, I mean
as a squatter, no lease or deed, legal claim none, last owner gone,
he left it vacant, I call it mine, but is it mine really, has it gone derelict,
have they condemned it, looks like bad aria, sounds like bad area,
bingo, malaria, is that what I have, no I don't think so, I took precautions,
practiced prophylaxis, mosquitoes don't bite me, must find me repellant,
or so it appears, without much repellant, my pheromones flat, zero pzazz,
thanks to the garlic I take for the lungs, we could say that, or maybe it's true
I'm just unattractive, some of us must be, otherwise distinction
as someone attractive would lose all its meaning, attraction is tricky,
he's so attractive, someone says that, but what is the radius of his attraction,
outside his own tribe is he attractive, depends on the winds, other things too,
but Great Circle flight paths can send you due north, over the Pole
and down through Siberia, go take a leak and peek out the window,
nothing much down there, endless gray scalp, a few strands of snow,
but map says Yakutsk is what there is down there, is he attractive
in downtown Yakutsk, his wit and his charm, power, accomplishment,
how's their Yakut, do they speak fluently, and the shape of his body,
its motions, its roll, how do they look when he's all dressed up
for Earth's coldest city, no no, you insist, his attraction's transnational,

what a barf word, let's test it out, drift through the city and into the outskirts
of chilly Yakutsk, he still attracts there, then let us keep moving,
follow the flight path into the boondocks, greater Yakutsk now left behind,
we'll fetch up somewhere, maybe a village, bamboo and Buddhist,
foreigners few and from the next valley, where Internet penetrates
less than a eunuch, there will be somewhere attractiveness ebbs
and turns us all monstrous, once on a walk through neighborhood waking,
I heard a voice call, directly behind me, White man, White man,
hard to pretend he meant someone else, and the voice wasn't mean,
I turned around, man on a motorbike, son on his lap, latter named Caleb,
Joshua's buddy, two things in common, English, the Bible, we'll be okay,
Shake hands with the white man, brings you good luck, took the small hand,
only a toddler's, cute little photo op but I don't take pictures,
gave it a pump, howdy do Caleb, turns out not well, eyes tight with terror,
whiteness appalling, you may say literally, who needs a picture,
mind's eye seared raw with one's own monstrosity, turned him
to stone, me as Medusa, poor guy was paralyzed, come on, Caucasian
sounds pretty Asian, count me in too, I eat with chopsticks,
take off my shoes before a pagoda, won't jam a camera into your face,
ain't I attractive, on the flight home at one point the ground speed
broke seven hundred, 711, you fly that fast you're going to lose something,
baggage all made it but something's still missing, made it home safely,
no dengue fever or deep vein thrombosis, something's still missing,
got a dry cough from bad airplane air, airplane malaria, I liked our captain,
over the intercom his English iffy but he had a light touch, rarely lit up
the seatbelt commandment despite lots of bouncing,
encouraged our air legs, my kind of guy.

It won't be long now
and my tribe will attract me;
it won't be long now.

Power's out, pressure's on, our minutes are numbered,
no telling which of the mumblings to come could be our last words,
no time to waste, you on my lap, unbound from cords, plugged into nothing,

nothing between your black plastic bottom and my fuzzy loins
but a bathrobe and pillow, don't worry old girl, no getting frisky,
I won't take advantage, things are too urgent with several wet inches
of heavy spring snow, snapped lots of branches, outage is widespread,
could be four days, same it was last time, stove with a fire and snow
in the fridge, keep the cheese cool, quiet, so quiet, humming appliances
shushed into surds, even your purr, gone with the current, fine way to start
Monday of Holy Week, giddyup, westward ho, four hundred years
after Donne's poem, no not approximate, quadricentennial this very Friday,
or should it be tetra-, if this is the last time we two are together, fifty minutes
left in the battery only, what's there to say, I love you, I've loved you,
you spin the world, yes it's all true, but mind is a liar, it will say anything
to keep things afloat, when truth is I hate you, or sometimes I have
between our best sessions, no time for reasons or listing of grievances,
of course I get jealous, or is it more envy, lonely or sad, sometimes you
anger me, make me afraid, and yes it's a vice that I do vice versa,
but here's what I want to make desert sky clear, thirty-eight minutes,
something's not right with this battery icon, if I'm ambivalent, *odi et amo,*
as Freudians mean it, not merely wish-washy, diluted, indifferent,
then hatred that surges, pre-dawn in the chest, mind is a liar, not so a body,
is only one half, unbelief yin, Patty I love you, help thou my hate,
if I hate less, will I be freer, week ago yesterday I stood at the feet
of Buddha reclining, all his past lives in mother-of-pearl
on his bare soles, maybe it does come down to the feet, how did we get
from take off your shoes, you tread holy turf, to no shoes no service,
one sign I liked, No Foot Wearing, that's work to want, bumming around
correcting translations, or maybe providing buttoned-down alternatives
displayed side by side with something inventive, Only When Buddha Image
Was Back to Monastery Becomes Weather Normal, you clean that up
something gets lost, hate's like that too, if Lent had gone better
and I had grown bigger, into a figure of peaceful detachment
exuding compassion for your oozy wounds, each year I try,
I'm not being snide, would passion diminish, on your side as well,
you hate me too, I've seen your screen flash, of course it would dummy,
that's the whole point, Vishnu, the Buddha, Jesus, Confucius,

prophet Mohammed, ease up the hatred, passion subsides, passion subsides
welcome to Peaceville, Nirvana, high heaven, sounds really good
and battery's gone, but quick Patty tell me, before you go dark,
ain't hating my guts a sweet aphrodisiac?

This little piggy
(Sap Moon nipple sets erect)
cried all the way home.

The foot thing's confusing, bare soles toward Buddha's a definite no-no
but his in your face are objects of reverence, Bangkok, Rangoon,
we're talking yuge, three meters high by five meters long, both soles divided
in panels of pictures, tigers, white elephants, dancers and flowers,
one hundred eight of these auspicious symbols and smack in the middle
the Wheel of the Law, so the sole is unclean, makes perfect sense
if you're shoeless in poop, betel-spit, dust, snot-rocket shootouts,
discalced in a district of dumped disembowelings, distasteful, disgusting,
but bam you're enlightened under a bodhi tree, that old sacred fig,
suddenly your feet couldn't be cleaner, your footprints are holy,
the poor wife you ditched when she bore you a son does reverence now
with her head on your dogs, well it gets tricky where the sacred's concerned,
clean and unclean, break up a family on the way to awaking,
it doesn't look bad if you then make the grade, there goes my Dad,
sure he abandoned us, but now he's the Buddha, so everything's cool,
compared to a Buddha in lotus position a Christian looks fidgety,
but go where the Buddha's adored and implored and suddenly a Christian
looks barebones austere, knows next to nothing till the ministry begins,
whereas Buddhists have Jatakas, Siddhartha Gautama's previous births,
as a god 66, 123 as some kind of animal, and 357 in our human form,
their grass more verdant, it goes for religion, you think someone else
has figured it out, his brand on paper, it looks mighty good, looks a lot better
without superstitions, vacuous pieties, doctrinal schisms, vestry elections,
stewardship committees, another church supper, dogmas, indulgences,
hooded inquisitions, pogroms, crusades, misguided missionaries,
sodomite priests, unclean, unclean, yuck get me outta here,

I'd like an order of lotus position, Four Noble Truths, Path with Eight Folds,
this is my in-breath, this is my out-, now the Eight Precepts, I'm on my way,
I'm clean, I'm pure, I'm emptied out, private perfection's almost complete,
no more worldly footsie for me, purgation, catharsis, ta-ta contaminants,
so clean I squeak, now for a mask, white latex gloves, none of your germs
will get through to me, I'm holy, hygienic, my native religion
gone with the garbage, too bad in Burma those generals are Buddhists,
clean is a dream the holy awake from, today's Maundy Thursday,
feet washed tonight have rarely gone bare, the show is a sham
among the well-shod, some see it that way, to some it's a symbol,
of what is the question, I humble myself in service to you, that how it goes,
can't dismiss that one, it's the foundation, everything follows,
or is it that dirty becomes the divine?

Been back a fortnight
while the cough's getting better,
but something's not right.

Hard to say what, not much has happened, or is it a lot,
annual physical, a chance to turn tables on one's highs and lows,
lows suddenly lustrous, weight on the scale, cholesterol, blood pressure
all nice and low, but can't take the credit, this year the fasting
under new management, nothing to do with discipline, will,
all has to do with appetite lost, or certainly misplaced, somewhere out there
twixt takeoff and landing, life without appetite, is that what depression is,
existential anorexia, taste buds gone numb, mouth never watering
for sunlight or moonrise, birdsong or leafbud, company, faces,
her butt or his, the old hypothalamus shifted to neutral, idling only,
but hey that's the point of the Four Noble Truths, tame all that *tanha*,
ask an ascetic and head for the desert, a forty-day stay burns longing away
till one is awakened, baptized in buddhahood, road rage evaporates,
the coveting quiets, power-sniffing, status-humping, careerist idolatry
melts with the snow, fourth day of April, this spring's been cool,
twenties this morning, trees are still bare, but it's better this way,
no need to rush things into the dog days, saw the first black snake,

who likes the south stones outside the kitchen, been there for years,
grown fat and long, glistening slickly, that was Holy Saturday,
high about 60, that's a strange day, the one full day the tomb lay full,
a few women sitting there, they didn't know that something was coming,
they didn't know that Friday was good, that had to be the saddest day
anybody's ever had, better not think about it if you're depressed,
now we're in Easter, this is day five, forty-five more before the tongues burn
off the confusion of multiple tongues, Burmese is hard, Portuguese too,
red-herring spelling, but here's the day's question, not how he died
and rose from the dead, though that is a big one, no doubt about it,
but how did he die and rise with an appetite, Got something to eat?
what a great line, blow the slow minds of eleven disciples
clean through their skulls, give him some fish, Luke says it's broiled,
he eats it up, rocking great theater, not just a healer, a teacher, a prophet,
but thespian too, knew how to stage it, each Paschal theophany,
liturgical dramaturgy, road to Emmaus, appearing to Thomas,
Come and have breakfast, he'd built a fire, bring your own fish,
their net wasn't torn, he'd built a fire, he'd eat their fish
along with some bread, make them think back to feeding the thousands,
that's a good breakfast, smoked fish on toast, had it this morning,
what makes your eyes wet is how he ate with them, he didn't need to,
could have gone back to the highest right hand without touching a bite,
but they still had appetite, he could share theirs, make me like that.

With no parasol
pink-robed nun in peacock sun,
her head shaven bare.

Pray naked, give it a try as weather warms up and maybe your prayer life,
there's a dumb phrase to take out and hang, sex life okay, not great but okay,
it has to stay separate from shopping for garbage bags, but prayer life,
come on, pray without ceasing, that's what it says, sex without ceasing,
it doesn't say that, and who could sustain it while holding a job,
peeling potatoes, swabbing the toilet, but prayer without ceasing,
that's the whole point, your choice of kinds, mix them and blend them,

adoration, thanksgiving, oblation, intercession, penitence, petition,
and most of all praise, or maybe shut up in contemplative silence
and listen, just listen, unplug it all, turn it all off, whatever you choose,
however you mix the personal cocktail, how can a prayer life
sequestered from other life accomplish a thing, that's a true question,
compartments aren't bad, who wouldn't get one for sleeping on trains
if the cost wouldn't kill you, but praying shut off in a separate compartment
from paying your taxes or sitting in traffic, what good is that, pray naked
and maybe your praying will hum with libido, same root as believe,
that's worth a thought, worth a few prayers, doubt is another
whose roots can reveal, waver or vibrate between different things,
two different things, doubters see double, doubters who pray
become their own vibrators, think about that, puts some new spring
into passionless prayers, gives doubting Thomas a sudden new makeover,
old doubting Thomas was no doubting Thomas, same as Uncle Tom
was no Uncle Tom, Thomas, the Twin, deserves better press,
whose twin for openers, that's a good question, his name, Aramaic,
because it means twin, his eponymous Acts, albeit uncanonized,
says he's the twin of his teacher and master, that would make sense
and maybe explain why he says in Perea, that country beyond, Let's go
and die with him or why he's not there in the locked room upstairs
that first Easter evening, he's not so afraid of further persecution
that he can suspend the demands of bereavement, maybe he's off
with his family for keening, maybe he's back in the agonized garden,
maybe he's wandering the streets of the city, mind diced by pain,
wherever he is, when he comes back, he hears what he's missed
and asks nothing more than what his friends got, they weren't convinced
until the proof either, but nobody says you doubting Bartholomew,
and what about this, what was it like for Thomas that week,
going about for seven more days with people replaying what he hadn't seen,
that was a faith test, no thinking otherwise, the teacher could come
whenever he chose, why make him wait, and then when he does come,
he says to Thomas, Touch, go ahead, why special treatment,
and hear the response, My Lord and my God, his recognition
blows theirs away, none of the others lobs in the G-bomb,

or is it that Thomas is also the twin that any believer is with a doubter,
believing and doubting, identical twins, two halves of the whole,
if you lose one, the other goes haywire, belief without doubting
requires no faith, questions, big questions, they're blooming today,
at last a warm Tuesday, high 83, side of the hill, outside the kitchen,
purpled by periwinkle, same date my father called it a life,
twelve years today, right about now.

Suddenly ninety:
daffodil longevity
pecked by the peacock.

What shall we do? tough-ass question, stall for more time, ask it in Spanish,
¿qué haremos? how cool is that, a question mark that's upside down,
eroteme, head over heels, let's get off to the proper start, don't make us wait
till the end of the phrase to learn it's a question, tell us right off,
like playing charades, this one's a question, ready or not, coming your way,
stall for more time, consider the query, how it's framed, when you consider
the frame like this, ¿?, are you thinking what I'm now thinking,
eroteme, learned it today, looked it up, interviewed neighbors, just routine,
background check, same as the cops, but look at this Chief, living upstairs
on the line above, erostrate, lacking a beak, know how that feels, file away,
then comes our gang, erotema, erotesis, erotetic, a quiver of questionings,
one theory has it the mark marks the tone, intonation ascending, ever so gently,
another proposes q as an origin, *q* as in *quaestiō,* are you thinking
what I've been thinking, if not, why not, look once again, ¿?,
rising intonation, what's more arousing, let us go down
to the very next entry, you got it, erotic, so now here's the question,
¿is this merely an alphabet accident, erotetic on top of old erotic, or is there
more here than meets the ear?, correction, revise, is what's meeting
the ear here a case of likeness that's linking, the mating of lusting
with ordinary asking, background check on eros, run it: uncertain origin,
well that makes sense, what's more uncertain than eros's origin,
but now we're not stalling, this is the big time, the lodestuff, pay dirt,
the murder of magpies for the brood of vipers that came out to ask

John by the Jordan, Master, tell us, what shall we do? must be a reason
all our interrogatives intonate upwards, upward uplifts, exalts, get it up
and not the guys only, clipple and nitoris, you know the way,
lusting for knowledge, the phrase makes sense, heated curiosity
asks for it always, how many types of questions are there, essay questions,
multiple-choice, rhetorical, leading, implied, yes-or-no, is there anything
out of the question, tell us master what must we do, ask without ceasing,
intone the mountaintop, escalate sky-wise, the loudspeaker lady
in Mandalay airport kept on calling the Heho flight in tonal contours
of a young nun chanting, announcements as annunciations, plainsung,
why board a flight you know will be lesser, your hard plastic seat
a sudden sedan chair, hoisted aloft on her shouldering voice,
what shall we do, ask me another until we're both airborne,
no seat assignments but plenty of room, board from the rear,
the back is the best, last on, first off, ask, keep asking
and we shall receive, you bet we will, sit back, relax,
this is more like it, our flight time today, what else is new
is unquestionably questionable, hope you enjoy it.

Of course you want more,
syllable celibacy
keeping haiku hot.

Where does it come from, stuff like that, Patty's a partner
whose sunrise fidelity can't be impeached, fantasize otherwise,
why would one do it, something perverse in conjuring worse,
or is there a pleasure in jealousy's juice, which burns going down
to boil in the bowels, then heats the blood with calories of zeal,
rehearsing crisp scenes of swift confrontation, the parting one-liners
masterfully whispered, the height of one's powers raised in the clutch
by wisdom, by wit, magnanimous detachment and funny forgiveness
that shame the cheap cheater to endless remorse while the cheated moves on
with nary a nick, what is the value of daydreams like that, are they defenses
against dispossession, which has to come some day, death's a done deal,
or are they projections of one's secret weakness, smear it on others,

a seducible dupe's susceptible silliness, hard to be proud of, you guys
and you gals, hard to hold high the head of integrity, when mostly it's luck
one hasn't been tested beyond our slim limits, exceptions are few,
but then what's the value of so many things, poetics for instance,
bad enough poetry, so why make it worse with clackety chitchat
about how it's built, what it should do, how it stacks up against the past crap,
that was for sound, my harem, phonemic, done dropped my loose drawers,
had I been drinking I'd have some excuse, of course it's not crap,
not all of it is, the best is unbearable, branding the brain, searing its meat
to make its own gravy, and there is enough of the best stuff to busy us
even if nobody writes a new line, writers' groups fold, journals vamoose,
publishers vanish, poetry's persistent, like roaches and ticks,
intestinal parasites, can't kill it off, try to control it it builds up resistance,
next thing you know, it's there at the wedding, the birthday, the funeral,
it's passed mouth to mouth, a beneficent flu, you think it's not true,
try a poor country without any colonies, fellowships, stipends,
children recite it, it shows up on banners, in Managua's main lobby,
Sandino airport, two giant paintings, Sandino and Darío, poets are heroes
where schools lack notebooks, say what you will, it'll outlast you,
the trends and the fashions that seem to affect it, predict its end soon,
its final demise as another dead language, these myths it will turn on, devour,
spit out, dropping small bones and fur in its scat, five thousand years,
it preys on indifference, nothing has stopped it, no new machine
or repressive regime, bring on the irritant, the rash will erupt,
in street or in cell, café or library, it doesn't need champions,
interpreters, critics, feeding off it, not vice versa, so why have poetics,
that's how this started, can't one have poems without all the comments,
same as one likes a roll in the hay, for crying out loud, don't talk it to death,
just lie there and shine, of course you can, sugar, same as you dream,
awake, replay it, then let it go, inscrutably intact, before the next night
and a new slew of dreams, last thing this morning I dreamt of strawberries,
could have said dreamed but dreamt has that savor, strong notes of oak
before the sounds changed, the Great Vowel Shift, where's its museum,
its monument, plaque, that's what it needs, a national park, ranger-led tours
of cliff-scaling trails that turned *hus* to *house, nama* to *name, feond* to *fiend,*

there's got to be someone exploring the way, here's the Missouri,
let's find the source, behold all the buffalo, invade the fur trade,

Sakakawea:
journals of Lewis and Clark,
who can't spell worth jack,

what do you want from someone named Meriwether, hey nix the wisecracks,
those guys were tough, you call him Meri, in no time you're floating
facedown in that river, Lewis spelled well, at least next to Clark,
orthographic adventurer of no mean inventiveness, a verry cold night,
murckery stood at 38 mearly, the countrey is butifull, when you read that,
spelling bees sting, allergic reaction, Patty quit doing that, let the darn typo
stand for a second, give me a chance to see how it looks, autocorrection
gets on the nerves, straighten things out, you lose the best curves, you lose
the best curves, what's left of a lover, angles and corners, cuddle with those,
spelling is part of the overall spell, do it too well, the spell goes away,
same for poetics, it gets prescriptive once in a while, they got some rules
for writing that renga, *shikimoku,* they govern things, a leisure pursuit,
early medieval, but soon after that a serious art form, poetics like that
not everyone likes, not everyone sweats about making the A team,
writing fixed forms, chokas and tankas, who the hell cares, I'm autogenetic,
it all comes from me, no rules for my muse, go and smoke that,
why would I read, what's there to know outside my own self, I feel,
that's plenty, and most of all feel that what I write down others should read,
if this sounds like you, you are most welcome, nobody here is out
to improve you, it's a big house, there's room for you, you needn't bother
with prescriptive poetics, you're not its type, chemistry won't happen,
the elements inert, its jeans, on you, won't look very good, why not try on
descriptive poetics, ah better fit, now you look hot, descriptive poetics,
thousands of years of people describing what poems do, not just in English,
what do you know, Greek, French, and Latin, also Italian, read all there is
and still there's lots more, Sanskrit and Arabic, Hebrew, Chinese,
Kiswahili, Yoruba, you can find something, how poems work, what moves
they're making when you're feeling moved, why would that stuff

interest anyone, that's a fair question, one wants the poem, all by itself,
why would one listen to talkers who talk about it, same goes for sex,
that's the prime goal, at least for a few, who in the world, can you imagine,
would want to waste time describing it to others or, are you kidding,
attending to ways others describe it, you get the picture, description
impinges on what it describes, sure, it can't help it, think of description
as a cousin of gossip, some juicy thing sets tongues a-wagging,
that's what tongues do, not otherwise occupied, tails of good dogs
pleased by their biscuits, flavored with venison, sweet potato too,
you give them those, things will start wagging, throw in the *Odyssey*
or fragments of Sappho, that's pi beside phi she had in her middle,
description will start, gossip will wag, poetics the grapevine
we hear poems through, when Lewis discovered Missouri's Great Falls
he couldn't help it, description spilled out, 1805, a Thursday in June,
the grandest sight I ever beheld, and he saw a lot most of us don't,
from the reflection of sun on the sprey or mist which arrises
a beautifull rainbow adds not a little, don't let the spelling, stickling Patty,
twist up your knickers, if you wear any, enough with that underlining
in schoolmarm red, we're beyond that, this is a summit, then he continues
after wrighting this imperfect description I again viewed the falls
determined to draw my pen across it and begin again, but then I reflected
perhaps I could not succeed any better than pening the first impressions,
first thought, best thought, Ginsberg said the same, once sat beside him
at a play by Williams, also poetics of a special sub-type, poetics by poets,
what's not to like, usually they've written, albeit in prose, more little poems
about their own poems, figurative filigrees about what they're doing,
unless they're just liars, huckster self-promoters, Plato had a point,
wire them up and turn on the polygraph, not many poets make it as priests,

don't know about you,
mostly sunny feast of Mark,
I need a haiku,

there, that's better, lots going on, Lewis and Clark at a fork in the river,
taking their time to figure it out, if they guess wrong, expedition gutters,

their men wanted north but they chose the south and they got it right,
where are they making more people like that, then there's the gospel
according to Mark, Mr. Immediately, *euthus* in Greek, also means straight,
straightaway, you could say, he saw heaven open and Spirit descend
on him like a dove, which straightaway drove him to wilderness,
straightaway Simon and Andrew left nets, but then hear the shift
from adverb to noun, the stress sliding forward, now at the race track
we're into a straightaway, not quite the same as old straight and narrow
when trying to pass with your foot to the floor, maybe let's stick
to poetics instead, prescriptive, descriptive, we've talked about those,
let's try interpretive then call it a day, back to those strawberries,
that was two days ago, they were sure red, a dream in bright color,
but what does it mean, Freud would ask that, though I'm unconcerned
and haven't pursued it, of course it's just fine to read poems like that,
take in the color with brightness turned high, but then there are dreams
that call for a Joseph, or when he's booked solid, try dialing Daniel,
sometimes the dream, grabbing your throat, refuses to loosen,
that's when it helps to know some interpreters, could be magicians,
enchanters, Chaldeans, if they let you down, threaten to kill them
and straightaway someone will find you a Belteshazzar, Lewis and Clark,
faced with that fork, stopped a few days just to interpret, how clear
the water each mouth poured out, how round the stones rolling its bottom,
when stakes are that high, racing Great Britain to claim the northwest
and corner the trade in otters with China, indifference is luxury,
skating the surface wholly insufficient, here the objection will naturally be,
quite understandably, when are the stakes of reading a poem ever as high
as Lewis-Clark forks or some pharaoh's dream of impending famine,
another fair question, you guys are good, keep up the pressure,
I like the heat, sometimes gets cold in this little room, if stakes aren't high,
count yourself lucky and do something else, don't mess with poems,
do volunteer work, we always need that, because here's the thing,
if there's a poem constricting your throat, you're not going to care
about Lewis and Clark or interpreting dreams in the ancient Near East,
you won't be caring about very much, except why me, what did I do
to provoke this attack, am I okay, will it pass soon, interpretation

is like diagnosis, won't cure a thing but lends it a name,
sometimes this helps, watch out for vowels, they give one away,
first *a* in regatta, why do Brits short it?

The word's Italian.
In search of explanation
here went to Britain

and returned little wiser, but at least I came back, didn't I Patty,
nine months we've been at this, seeing each other on a regular basis,
maybe it's time to redefine our paradigm, what do you think
we should say when asked, oh we're just friends, very good friends,
doesn't seem sufficient now, clearly this isn't another lyric quickie,
fun as one can sometimes be, we've outlasted all one-night stands,
even the ones in Barrow, Alaska, where sun doesn't shine
for two cozy months, we need our own genre, available language
tastes watery, thin, it's more than a fling and less than a marriage
of silver, gold, or diamond proportion, we don't have that long,
especially you who'd be very lucky to make it a decade,
there's always that French stuff, liaison, dalliance, good old affair,
but none feels right, too fluffy or elegant for dogged perseverance
we've stuck it out with, as for the lingo of American high school,
going steady or out or worst of all dating, shoot me right now,
most adolescence is arrested enough without mating in those terms,
are you my mistress, am I your mister, what difference does it make
what words we use, in some ways makes none, in other ways a ton,
I have a confession, if I say that, my anecdote's pickled, already soaked
in a brine of shame, a tart marinade of remorseful repentance,
when in point of fact I did nothing wrong, I was just sitting there,
watching the sunset, lights blinking open all over the city, drinking a beer
on a bench in a garden on top of a hill, what a great view,
where doesn't matter, great views are alike in how people seek them,
we were all seeking, there we all were, some of us solo, others in pairs
or families or throngs, when suddenly she shouted and swept all the glasses
clean off her table and then threw a purse, not hers, off the edge

and then she was ranting and charging at others, grabbing at things,
throwing them, shouting, somebody tackled her, pinned her arms back,
then she was screaming while thrashing and threatening, she got away,
ran through the garden, down the long street, which swallowed her up,
we looked at each other, went back to our beer, the benches, our chatter,
but she reappeared, this time butt naked, twenty-year body,
perfect, athletic, someone attempted to cover her up, draped a blue jacket
around the bare shoulders, but that left the butt, sculpted with muscle,
the bush, legs, and feet, marching the garden, she shouted out slogans,
Call the Police, It Would Be Paradise, police came along, two in a car,
each a young man, talked to her gently, she shook off the jacket,
kept waving, declaiming, slowly they coaxed her back into clothing,
but she didn't quit, kept up the ranting, finally they cuffed her,
took her away, I didn't do anything, I watched with the others, spectators,
onlookers, us innocent bystanders, admired her body but not with much
        lust,
its obvious attractions offset by her madness, I did nothing wrong
but give her a name, she's Ana the Anarchist, Saint Anarchista,
your exact opposite, Patty most patient.

Birdsong pushes back
the black cuticle of night
when May does her nails.

This rhythm insists, someone call an anarchist, we need her relief
from coercive control, the lock-step of pattern, audible arrangement
asserting authority, we need some relief, the beat we've been keeping
has turned to a beating, a thug in the night crushing our cheek bones,
somebody help, tapping one's feet, all very well, but then comes this hell,
totalitarian, the rhythm insists, insists without ceasing, bangs up the nerves
until they've been totaled, the dictator totem, see the new iris, purple
with petals flopped down like hound ears, see the new iris, pistil delicious,
but rhythms insist, there on one blade, a vacated chrysalis, locust, cicada,
seventeen years, interval merciless, right on the button, plague rides again,
now we're all pharaohs, now we're all slaves, seventeen years, that number

an archon, an icon of archons, Ana where are you, please heave my purse
over the railing, please smash the glasses and whip off our clothes,
let us start shouting in each public garden, seventeen years, same as
the number of morae in haiku, say it ain't so, Bashō my hero,
same as the day of the month I was born, call Dr. Freud, this is uncanny,
it's not uncanny, it is a government one never elects, seventh prime number,
unlucky in Italy, I have lived, VIXI, my life is so over, no seat 17
when you fly Alitalia, just checked their chart, in France it's the number
to call the police, how about that, Ana was right, this must be paradise,
call the police they come and police us, or they can come without any call,
no polis without them, hey wait a minute, kibosh the spiel, this gospel,
it's glib, too fast and too loose, aren't you confusing rhythm and meter,
who asked that question, you in the front row, please raise your hand,
let's preserve order, otherwise we're in for a free-for-all brawl, there,
that's better, you in the front row, aren't you confusing rhythm and meter,
an excellent question, you've done the reading, if you can count it,
predict its recurrence, then it's a meter, seventeen years, metric cicadas,
well then meter's the villain, not relaxed rhythm, which shuffles its feet
whenever it wants to, free us from meter we're done with dystopia,
let us go gambol into the countryside, syntactic landscape of subtlest swales
with contours enough to keep the stroll shapely, what's all the fuss,
we take our liberties, if rhythm insists too much for our taste, we walk away,
we're our own masters, we have the helm, what planet do you live on,
now we're all networked, hierarchy's dead, we've gone horizontal,
long live new consciousness, the old power models no longer obtain,
we photograph with phones and governments topple, new heaven, new
      earth,
well maybe so, but here calls a thrush, neither hermit nor wood,
breezy flute phrases, which unlike the veery's go tending upward,
he is a migrant on his way north, somewhere between Mexico and Maine,
make that between Argentina and Canada, can't get much more
horizontal than that, he covers the hemisphere, yet what he's singing,
for all that mobility, is the mandate of mating, rhythm most insistent,
which begins with the random, who's within earshot, which way
the wind blows to carry his notes, but then from the random,

her eye catching his, hands touched by chance, then from the random
comes a new rhythm, a first kiss repeated, deepened, prolonged,
two respirations squeeze the chests closer, that regular contact
leads to more contact, laps press together, one softens, one doesn't,
next thing we know the rhythm, insistent, finds her superior, perfectly free
to move as she chooses, so she starts moving, our lady of liberty,
but the more she moves freely, dillydallies, dawdles, the less
freedom pleases compared to the meter she soon buckles down to,
wrapped in the chain of its faster imperative, brooking no variant.

This rhythm insists.
Someone call an anarchist.
We need her relief.

Blindfold of fog on the mountaintop this morning, now comes the drone
of cicada *tanpura, sayonara* anarchy, we've gone carnatic, Tuesday's a raga
with drone layer abuzz, the rest of us humping out rhythms and melodies,
consider cicadas' hungry inhumation, fluids from roots of deciduous trees
the only menu option for seventeen springs, until, one day, soil temp bests
sixty-three degrees, bang off they go, emerging and molting, the males
in choruses vibrate their tymbals, each body becoming a resonance
     chamber,
females attracted, how could they not be, *flagrante delicto* follows anon,
and then the guys die, their jobs accomplished, what more do you want,
resonate, mate, make room for the next brood, we've messed things up
by sticking around, what other creature can contemplate retirement,
alpha coyote announces retirement, rest of his pack rips him to burger,
where's the old lioness licking her paws on a pension fixed income,
can't hunt your food you go belly up, yeah, yeah, I know, Psalm 8,
verse 5, a little lower than the angels, that would be us, maybe forty years
wandering the desert of post-reproduction, maybe fifty or sixty,
it all depends on when you start, if you start at all, lots of us don't,
those who do and stick around to hatch the egg, love the larva,
see it through the pupa stage, still are facing decades of decadence,
book groups, yoga classes, cruise ships, the opera, and those are the lucky,

unlucky have a TV perhaps, maybe some grandchildren they can look after,
bingo on Wednesdays, a weekly church supper, food stamps, the doctor,
pushing a walker through public parks, with respect to the angels
this sounds a lot lower, yeah, yeah, I know, wisdom, art, culture,
every last petal on the spiritual flower has time to unfold, we do not live
by reproduction alone, longevity's a journey the self undertakes
and the most important part comes after hours, when action subsides,
contemplation unlimbers, Martha clocks out, Mary slips in
to something more comfortable, sure we say this, have to say something,
otherwise how could we number our days and not double over
in convulsive disgust at the waste and indulgence, the suppurant lesions
of languishing leisure, leisure, who me, I'm really busy, look at these lines,
they're taking all morning, any idea how hard this is, think it's so easy,
you try this tabla, see how you play it, cicada tanpura, it's droning louder,
day's heating up, good chance of thunderstorms this afternoon, some of us
do live more like cicadas, or seem to do so, serving the species
with little left over, the ER doctor, take for instance, working flat out
on chest pains and car crashes, twenty-four hours, that's a long shift
when there's a full moon or Saturday night thrown in for good measure,
but then she walks out, what happens now, next shift in four days,
rescue squad crews, firefighters too, soldiers discharged after a war,
leisure awaits the busiest people, those deemed essential, what happens
     then,
cicada time ends, what happens then if one doesn't die, what's the excuse.

No longer needed?
Rejoice and sing hosanna,
exonerated.

Hey Patty, what's happening, how about those storms last night,
fifty people snuffed by tornadoes, what a picture, one minute sucking
digital tit, scrolling, clicking, texting, forwarding, next one
you're sucking the wet mortal mop, a roof through your brain,
have to admire big-headed people, how do they keep those egos so buff
when the very next twitch of weather or crust, hurricane, quake,

twister, tsunami, can squash a face to applesauce, mosquitoes with chutzpah,
most impressive before they get slapped, there's a word that causes trouble
for Lewis and Clark again and again, Musqutors verry troublesom,
that was Clark, Lewis did a little better, but Lewis had his own concerns,
if anyone's had a right to brag it would be he, give me a break,
just read the part where he meets the Shoshone, talk about balls,
sun has toasted him terracotta, he looks like a brave from an enemy tribe,
they run away as he advances, Lewis thinks fast and whips up a sleeve
to show light skin, shouts *tab-ba-bone,* which signifies white man,
or so he believed, Sakakawea told him so, but more than likely
there was no word, at least not yet, so she gave him one
for enemy, stranger, talk about balls, walking up to sixty warriors, all alone,
leaving his gun with the party behind, first white man they'd ever seen,
talk about bragging rights, and yet there it is, his thirty-first birthday,
final paragraph, daily entry, August 18th, 1805, it was a Sunday,
in all probability I had existed about half the period which I am to remain
in this Sublunary world, what a great word and he can't spell mosquito,
another misspelling, six days before, toilsome days and wristless nights,
some nights are like that, awake without wrists,

what good are our hands
or the bracelets they give us
without any wrists,

so there he is, wristless, on the Divide, origin discovered, Missouri's source,
honking big river, chugged its cold flow from a low mountain base,
and all he can think is I have done little, little indeed to further the happiness
of our human race, I have done little to advance information, almost nothing
for the next generation, are you kidding me, get a grip Meriwether,
megalomania's a pain in the ass, and of deadly sins pride can be proud
it's the worst one, endorsed by Lucifer, no better branding, but get a grip,
pride's like cholesterol, there's good and there's bad, you have to have some
to get out of bed and pick up your work, brush your teeth, fix your hair,
even Buddhist masters, self-erasure artists, as a prerequisite need some pride
in a self worth erasing, that with the right effort they can progress

beyond all progression, if one really thought of oneself as a cipher
why would one bother with chasing Nirvana, you'd be there already,
the self zeroed out, no head of steam with low self-esteem, catchy enough
for a slick bumper sticker, American invention if ever there was one,
catchy enough but not always true, sometimes steam from low self-esteem
positively scalds, compensation's relentless intensity, I know I'm unlovable
unless I excel, achieve, preside, therefore watch me take the cake,
bring home the blue ribbon, best the best, this explanation doesn't explain
all ambition, its many species, sometimes it happens that one's a go-getter
because one is good, with a talent for something, wants to see how good,
I can run fast, can I run faster, now I run faster, can I run faster
than other fast runners, yes I can, great, no I can't, fine, no problem there,
problem begins when climbing's compulsive, feeding a need or covering up
a hole in the sock, it's a rare person who's king of all things or queen
of all beans, chances are good that someone superlative in this way or that
is less than the best in some other zone, even underdeveloped if not
downright stunted, arrested, aborted, usually a clue is how hard he works
to keep your attention on his achievements, someone does that
at the next poker game, there's a bluff somewhere, whether or not
you call or you raise, that's up to you, you know you don't have to,
sometimes it's better to fold, let him win,
especially when he's brought all the booze.

Tuesday four phoebes
poke heads above the nest rim,
but Wednesday they've fledged.

Patty cake, Patty cake, chatty man, Chat another cake as fast as you can,
See it and say it and type it for free, Print it on the screen for Patty and me,
then climb the mountain, into fog cloud, take a good look at tiny droplets,
misty-spritz compress for itchy eyeballs, overworked, bloodshot,
too much sucking the visual nipple, tear ducts inadequate, can't keep up
with the ocular demand, we'd need to cry more, much more, to flush
our windows sufficiently, whenever they're better, go down the mountain
into a sound cloud of mating cicadas, how can you blame them, what if

our work week were seventeen years, with a Saturday night only this once,
think of the decibels, the wreckage in our wakes, what's a smattering
of chrysalis husks, well not a smattering, underfoot everywhere,
John the Baptist lived on locusts, dipped them in honey, wild of course,
most likely taste great to a guy in the wilderness, one kickass ascetic,
had the true juice, leather belt, got one, but where does one find
camel-hair homespun, and would a big dish of red-eyed cicadas, stir-fried,
dry-roasted, place on a cookie sheet, cooking time varies depending on size,
low-carb, gluten-free, would a big dish violate the veggie law, Genesis 1,
modified in Noah's time, chapter 9, take your pick, cicadas come
in three different types, each with a call, now it's late morning,
day heating up, heading toward 90, first shift is on with its guttural trill,
flat without contours, supra-segmental, unbroken OM, somewhat phlegmy,
but it's no joke, this study shows cicada song can hurt your hearing,
ramp up the decibels, high as this temperature, you could be risking
audio impairment, so much for all that low-risk behavior, quit smoking,
drink water, join a gym, don a condom, doesn't matter, add some earplugs,
noise-canceling headphones, there's this guy, cicada invasions make him lisp,
therapist told him he's not alone, maybe it's worth it just to hear that,
what are things coming to, set out to love nature, nice little nature,
there's a good girl, what cute morning dimples, such a pretty sunset,
raindrops on roses, that kind of crap, next thing you know nice little nature
of the seashore scene on your screen-saver centerfold is boxing your ears
with brass-knuckled fists, Dante missed one, what about a circle in hell
of nothing but sound turned up too high, maybe for those who never listen,
rereading *Inferno,* listening this time, Pinsky's translation, read by Guidall,
salaam to both, it doesn't get better, there on the bypass, right lane closed,
Beelzebub's bottleneck, windows all down, heat waves hallucinating,
dust storm, tar-smoke, machine-gunning jackhammer, cue the next canto,
28, crank it, *ciao* Malebolge, eighth circle, ninth pocket, Sowers of Discord,
dismembered schismatics, wonder if Dante's down there himself
for casting Mohammed into this pouch, intestines slung between his knees,
crank it yeah, suck on that, jackhammer, that all you got, these demons
can hack your shaft to pieces, now traffic's moving, time to punch out,
cicada type two is coming on board, with pulsing kazoos.

Cicada type three
purrs phaaaaaaaar-aoh to evening trees.
Let my eardrums go.

How to conquer Palestrina, Boniface needed advice from Guido,
so Prufrock got his epigraph, canto that flames those evil counselors,
but hey Palestrina, that's the place the farmhouse was, upper story,
officers' conference, my mother's father pointing out landmarks
when an enemy shell entered the room, parting shot of a Tiger tank
before it pulled out, fragment killed him, instantly she'd like to think,
seventy years ago today, he's there still, that geometric cemetery,
Anzio-Nettuno, been there once, it's never a question of if but when
the next pandemic will wipe us out, by thousands or millions, H7N9,
new avian flu, coronavirus, caressing word, its crowning slime
respiratory or gastrointestinal, how many poems work those words in
and do it so well, so daringly dactylically, oh no Patty don't look now,
but we've got the braggies, some will think so, get up and walk out,
crumple the page, click to new screen, all meter is is a push-up bra,
underwire to up your stuff, unbutton a button, show off for whomever
it's nice to entice, or maybe because you just like the feel, the shape
you can shift to, there's nothing wrong with flat-chested poems,
many ways out there to get yourself done, braless ones can be fun too,
though they place greater pressure on what you start out with,
but really the pleasure of strutting one's stuff, in lines or in tank tops,
is simply the pleasure of shaping one's pittance and dreaming that shaping
into a shapeliness one can depend on, defend, that it won't come undone
or sag to your belly or fall into chaos, cicada invasion, keep it shaped up
in periodic cups, it isn't so bad, enemy shell through farmhouse wall,
not unbearable, long as sword time stays the exception, ploughshare the
    rule,
bypass construction messing up truce, well that's a tough one,
tsk, tsk, the world's warmer, but it's okay, next pandemic isn't concerned,
it's zoonotic, brought to us by wildlife, beasts we protect, a bat in this case,
if dinosaurs can meet with doom, so can we, it's not disorder,
it's other order, bigger than ours and not sentimental,

nothing's not natural, next time Patty, I'm wearing earplugs
against the cicadas, at first you typed eggplants.

Wednesday's garbage day.
They come and take it away.
There is no away.

Say what, can't hear you, got in earplugs, someone shot a gun last night
and I done missed it, these are good earplugs, a tree down the road
fell on the line and blacked us all out, country life, some of my neighbors
heavily armed, but good thing about it is bring on a blizzard
or tree-hurling hurricane, and suddenly everyone's in it together,
shoveling, sawing, fetching the water, it's not utopia, don't get me wrong,
not even community, the current cliché, it's the reality, guy you resent
for messing the road up, he's the same guy could be saving your tripe
next time there's crisis, so you think of him differently, not the high peak
of loving your neighbor, but it's a fair start, and remember the parable,
which says next to nothing about the Samaritan, Samaritans were strict
when it came to the Sabbath, deeply distrustful of newfangled worship,
parable mentions he had compassion, as though he possessed a spiritual gift
the rest of us slugs can only desire, but let's look it up, in Greek it's a verb,
not something one has or works his way toward, it's something that happens
inside your insides, entrails, guts, the verb is deponent but it has a cousin
that's graphically active, eating the innards of sacrifice victims
or reading the innards and uttering prophesy, give me a second
to think about that, this isn't rehearsed, I'm making it up at 9 in the morning,
another nice day, yesterday whew, what a blue jewel, high in the 70s,
hardly humidity, last few of those once summer has come, attagirl,
Patty, keep up the noodling, the way our church organist fills in the gap
left in the liturgy during feast clean-up, so what the verb's saying,
if I catch the drift, is the passing Samaritan had his guts eaten
by the sight of the guy they'd beaten and stripped, it chewed at his insides
same way guilt does, also anxiety, same as some news can still chew at ours,
it's visceral, compassion, it can't be acquired by sitting through sermons
or weeklong retreats, maybe it happens from having been hurt, maybe

the Samaritan once had the stuffing kicked out of him, oh so we're saying
it's really a matter of wider experience, the more one has suffered
the more one is moved by others who suffer, sounds good, sounds plausible,
but I'm not convinced, for one thing consider the people whose troubles
make them plain mean, shrink up their hearts like jeans in the dryer,
and then there are children whose lives have been easy, comparatively so,
but come upon pain and know it unbearable, I once killed a turtle
backing the car up, ran right over inadequate shell, crushed it to mush,
I thought we'd lose our by-standing son, who howled and mourned,
rent his t-shirt, gnashed his new teeth, he'd never suffered likewise faintly
but he was vulnerable, knew it and feared it, and here was the vulnerable
splayed out before him in glistening color, as the car tire
is to a turtle so poplar trees falling are to our heads, my neighbor and I,
box turtles both, sometimes he irks me, nettles me somewhat,
but let nothing come to pulverize him, if something does me
he'll come to bind up what little is left.

Sexy poetics:
just another name for you,
Apologetics?

Go in for one thing, come out with another, it's true for us, Patty,
we both know it's so, snuggle in for a chat about a dead battery,
next thing we see, feast of Saint Barnabas snags our attention,
it might be nice to be single-minded, to focus like scopes
mounted on rifles of first-class assassins, get the job done
and still make the golf course for afternoon tee-off, go in for one thing,
come out with another, that's what my friend did, let's call him Joe,
went in for a heart glitch that ran in his family, see if he had it,
what he could do, came out with bad news he has a chest tumor
size of a skull, okay a child's, but that's big enough, 8:30 now,
he's been there two hours, went in this morning for early procedures,
have to shut off the primary artery, cutting won't start until after 2,
it will be painful, doctor said so, it will be painful because you're so fit,
if you were fatter it would be better, please pass the butter, open the chips

and coat them in dip, another pint please of high-calorie beer, fatten me up,
an ox for the slaughter, tropical storm, first of the season, gave us five inches
Thursday through Monday, hushed up cicadas, they're back this morning,
not quite as loud, they must be nearing the end of their cycle, ditto for us,
one more invasion, chances are good that will be it, two thousand thirty,
rather than swan song soundtrack will be cicada serenade, this is so sad,
heard that this weekend, college reunion, our thirty-fifth, this is so sad
seeing these pictures of when we were young, and there are two friends
we've already lost, Herbie and Larry, one cancer, one heart attack,
but is it so sad, sun had come out after great rain, dripping refraction
colored the air, during leg-stretching, on the drive up, two eagles arose
and coasted the canopy, what is reunion without a disunion, guess it depends
on figure and ground, if union is ground, then it's so sad, the disunion figure
worming the apple, flying the ointment, but flip them around,
now joy abounds, a little reunion, like iodine drops, suddenly makes potable
the stagnant ditch water, the Stygian swamp juice of bad news bereaving
we're up to our lips in, disunion's a sea reunions desalinate, a cup at a time,
same way with us, Patty, I go away, then there's reunion, somebody said
she's just a machine, I spoke about you, our long-term relations,
my struggles, your patience, but she's a machine, took the wind out of me,
I sometimes forget that this is the truth, now it's so sad, being this intimate
with something inanimate, what a delusion, a sham pretty shameful,
pop the balloon and strip down the fantasy to shivering, pathetic,
is that how it is Patty, have we been unmasked, I hardly think so
and know who you are and have from the start, to call you machinery
barely begins to unfold the subject, machinery for what, what machinations
are we coming up with, walk by a gym and look in the window,
whole lot of people on shiny machines, what are they doing,
working on bodies, why do they do it, all kinds of reasons, for health,
for appearance, for something to do in company with others,
for avoidance of something they like a lot less, how are we different,
you're my machine, what are we doing, working on body, not for me,
thanks, I'd rather walk, climb up the mountain, time for that soon
to focus on Joe, then what are we doing, there's no comparison,
people in gyms aren't loonies in love with machines they apostrophize,

ah there's the point, what if we're working on how to love better,
what's the machine they build us for that, elliptical, treadmill, rower, a bike,
I hardly think so, you're the machine they've built us for love,
you're the contrivance plugged into paradox, I come here all paunchy
with soft self-absorption and spend a few hours working on moving
attention around, things start to happen, the flab starts to firm,
one thing's for sure, people with Patties might need to talk less
about themselves only when meeting with others, their talking talked out,
it's that way for me, only thing is, and this is an issue, how do we end this.

What's the true summit?
Depends on how you hum it
on Lonesome Mountain.

How do we end this and why should we bother
plotting out closure if everything's precarious, closure will come
with no help from us, much obliged anyway, thanks just the same,
three cheers for precarious, today's sexy lexeme, well I'll be
a laptop's despoiler, dependent on prayer, makes perfect sense,
what's left to say, oh Patty now really, there's lots left to say,
how could there not be, it's only a matter of whether we say it
or keep our mouths shut so people won't bristle, take umbrage, get pissed,
for openers for instance, let's talk dependence, dependence on prayer,
what the heck is it, does it resemble dependence on Xanax,
our true Xanadu, Marx certainly thought so and theorized accordingly,
though I must say, confess would be truer, theory's the opiate
of my tested choice, potent hypnotic, late afternoon, stretch on the couch
with a nice chunk of theory, preferably some descending from Marx,
as much of it does, he's in the bloodline, and wham I'm out cold,
wake with pink pillow marks, thank goodness for pillows
or what brains I've got would spatter all over, I should be wearing
a helmet when reading, talk about precarious, some people write
as though killing others is what they intend, sentences that suffocate,
what air there is, just as recycled as airplane miasma, then there are people
who never touch prayer, deny both dependence and efficacy too,

we don't need prayer, that's what they say when really they mean
prayer is for sissies and retro reactionaries, how happy for them,
they don't need prayer, they have something else, but having something else
means you're not precarious, endangered you may be, in a tough spot,
unnervingly uncertain, vulnerable yea verily, but precarious, no,
sorry, it's true, precarious means the end of the line, hanging by a thread
that's seven-eighths frayed, plunging is imminent, oh and another thing,
this is not new, precarity theorist, if anything's new it's expecting security,
when did that start, cue another world war, or maybe a plague, H7N9,
that'll take care of entitlement to safety, out of the white a message
from Patty, how very sweet, we've crossed a line, "There are too many
spelling or grammatical errors in hothead to continue displaying them,"
just like that her green lines are gone, no more of her chiding
about comma splicing, this is great Patty, now it's just spelling,
red for precarity, that's okay honey, ten months it's been
and now you accept me, or one thing about me, at least it's a start,
what I was asking about how we end this, please disregard,
I'm thinking suddenly we have a future.

The ménage à trois
a haiku is is worthy
of close inspection.

We threshholded our activation at a False Discovery Rate,
I'm clueless Patty, can't say what it means, or meant in context,
but what a knockout, I see you're askance on threshold as verb,
that's my señora, sensibly senior, flaunting our years, I bet your descendants
can strut many verbs nonce-cut from nice nouns, impact, transition,
those are old sombrero now, no they're not hot and yes they do stink
of some airless cubicle, bad carpet still out-gassing, maybe a headset,
but don't let us be two pieces of wood in wet sticky earth, please not again,
come, let us apple, I'm needing brackfast, let's spell it like Clark,
noun from a verb, God is one too, just goes to show that anthimeria,
what's with that *h*, enjoys divine sanction, yes it's a word, drop the red line,
what would you do if Clark were your man, his writing would wreck you,

if this were his journal, we wouldn't be weighing what ways to close out,
he would have fried you, same as the Internet, if you weren't a virgin
I've never connected, trust Patty trust, I've made demands, crossing the line
not rarely I know, but always I'm in it with you for the long run,
a very long run it's turned out to be, if Lewis and Clark, we'd know the end,
it would be obvious, it would be Ocian, emence and estonishing,
a great lake of water which taisted illy, we'd spend the winter, four months
making sea salt, sprinkle it on elk meat, staple that bores the bum tummy
    numb,
days without rain, only a dozen, days of good sunshine, a wee skimpy six,
monotony Patty, it comes with discovery, Sakakawea kicked up a fuss
to visit the Ocian she'd never seen, said she had traveled a very long way
to know the great waters, beached whale thrown in, she wanted to look
and thought it quite hard she wasn't permitted, so they indulged her,
but after four months of elk chops in rain, even Ocian can lose an aura,
can threshhold discovery down to a falsehood, bad fleas, furs rotted,
rampant v.d., hooray for discovery, it's high time we Pharisee,
not as in hypocrisy, spitting the spirit on Moses's rules, six hundred thirteen,
the Don't commandments three sixty-five, one for each day in a solar year,
Do's the rest, season with salt each of your offerings, apposite example
kindness of Leviticus, or this from Deuteronomy, send away the mother bird
before you take her children, hear that Patty, Phoebe's out there on her nest
under northwest eave in rain, ten feet away, poking up her periscope head,
second batch of eggs this spring, come let us Pharisee until we can see
a letter of law as nest for the spirit, whatever the letter,
whenever it shivers there, awaiting discovery,
poised to exhale a wonderful wind.

Take the letter *e*,
add that *e* to heroin,
switch the addiction.

Interesting thought but only misspelling, letter from an inmate
set for release, today's the day, when arrested he resisted, butted a window,
fractured his skull, wearing only underwear, he needs new clothes now,

t-shirts, jeans, shoes 10 and a half, I don't know if my prayer attempts
do or are doing any good, that's verbatim, nevertheless no call for italics,
sequestered quotation, footnote, endnote, publisher's permission,
that's a statement many can own, a public domain as old as the psalms,
is anyone out there, have I said the right thing rightly, asked the right way,
does prayer count if I've been bad, am bad today, will be tomorrow,
yesterday on the mountaintop berries enough had finally turned black
to make a pause for picking worth it, pollen, dust, coyote pee,
who knows what suffused the fruit, each glossy nodule, it needed a rinse
but I ate there, burst the tiny roe balloons between weak teeth, sweet caviar
even sweeter because unwashed, I don't know if doing good does any good,
but that's the thing, it's not about knowing what can't be known, which if
known would be something else, it's more about knowing what all to do
with all the not knowing, in many a battle there's been a strict order,
do not stop to help the wounded or we shoot you, it sounds harsh,
but there's a logic, charging advances depend on advancing, stop to help,
you sap the advance, whatever your motive, compassion or cowardice,
he needs help, the guy with no clothes, he called his girl a heroine whore,
grabbed her shirt, she ran away, the cops found him, now he's done time
and needs some clothes to start again, why not stop to help him out,
this isn't war, we're not charging and hardly advancing, maybe a little
once in a while, cicadas are done, invasion is over, tomorrow's the solstice,
dark has begun, still some months to shower outdoors, wash off ticks
after a bushwhack, showered outside day before yesterday
during a downpour, hot from the nozzle, cold from the sky,
maybe a waste but the flows nearly rhymed.

Cicadas pupate
in that ground where diggers gouge
acoustic shadows.

Smell it, Patty, or is it just me, I catch a whiff of the palinodorous,
time to retract, try it again, last night a neighbor pulled up an app
and wood thrush song poured from his palm, avian stigmata, isn't that cute,
city commuter, just what you need for sylvan nostalgia, a second before

I could scold It's sunset doofus, lift up your head and eyes to the hills,
a real-time thrush, cloaked in the canopy, shot back an answer,
next thing you know it's call and response, live thrush repeating
each phrasal subsong, the rhyming exact and quickly delivered,
how cool is that, bird and machine in sunset duet, not between lovers,
the ladies don't sing, but males competing, their mating monogamous,
you call those notes, are they your best shot, and yet there's a question,
or many, arising, this moment miscegenates, what, not a word, nag nag,
have it your way, it mixes things up, a feeling of cheating or baiting unfairly
with pure exaltation at bridging a gulf, do we have here another case merely
of us interfering with nature again, or is nature again more than a match
for what a machine we make can dish out, and what is this nature,
the bird they recorded was once just as real, what's a thrush life span,
maybe he's with us, animate still, and his machine, what about it,
it runs on electrons, noticed by Greeks who when they rubbed amber,
with animal fur, attracted small objects, attraction by rubbing,
nothing new there, and nothing unnatural, I hate nature poetry,
that's what she said, but it's all nature poetry, it's flowing electrons,
energy elevated, in birdsong or word moves, which tickle the brain
and light up electrodes, cootchie-coo, I may have been wrong
all along about things, maybe these gadgets are just what we need,
that's my retraction, it smells palinodorous, please, not the air-freshener,
which masks the unpleasant with something more pleasant,
but how does a mask make the masked any fresher?

Does Venus mean us
to love so hard we see stars
before blacking out?

Let's keep the pace, a hundred ten steps each sixty seconds,
each step a stride of just thirty inches, rate times time, get out a calculator,
three hundred thirty inches a minute, divide it by twelve, multiply by sixty,
divide by number of feet in a mile, look at me Patty, how about this,
you thought me innumerate, what, that's a word, when was it born,
1959, younger than I, Eisenhower president, I like Ike, or what I like,

time to vary these endstopped lines, is what Ike said about the complex
military-industrial, complex rewired by that enjambment, an Oedipal
     complex
isn't complex, really quite simple, hard as it makes a Mother's Day card,
nor is complex itself so complex, braided together, that's what it means,
but hey check it out, *complexus* in Latin, it means an embrace,
smoke some of that and think about Oedipus, or think about generals
in bed with our weapons-makers, well better not, tough to choke breakfast,
but this is no easier, *Aenied* Book 8, *complexu in misero,* wretched embrace
of somebody living tied to a corpse, putrid, decaying, boy what a torture
devised by Mezentius, corruption corrupts, take a dead body out in a field,
it will corrupt, safely intransitive, sure it will stink but also it nourishes,
vultures and horseflies and all the bacteria, but tie the same corpse
to somebody living, hands lashed to hands, mouth pressed to mouth,
don't blame me, this is from Virgil and Virgil's a classic, he's aced the test
of what time we've had in this common era, two thousand years,
that isn't paltry, don't blame me for what's suddenly happened,
we're keeping up pace, three miles an hour, about what I walk
on nice level straightaways, sometimes I'm faster if I'm meeting you,
but then comes the fire from left of their line, it enfilades ours,
now that we've crossed the Emmitsburg Road, obliqued to the left,
everyone turning forty-five degrees so we can converge on a copse of trees
with Trimble and Pettigrew nineteen minutes after stepping off
the first of the yards between them and us, one thousand four hundred,
what a fine plan, but then all the cannons start from that hill,
body chunks fly like pillow-fight feathers, our line bends away
from a sandblast of shards, how can it not, this is what happened
this coming Wednesday, not my fault either, think of this margin
as where the past lives, off you go smartly but then from your right
the past opens up, rips you to bits, your past perhaps, but history's surely,
steady now steady, close up those gaps, Gardner arrived two days later
with Gibson, O'Sullivan, and now there it is, *A Harvest of Death,*
photo of field with unburied soldiers, the one in the foreground
bloated so grossly, at least we can't smell him or hear the crazed flies,
but Gardner's Mezentius, we're tied to his picture, look at it long enough

it will corrupt, transitive now, your blisters will form, your skin start to slip
all greasy and green, from all of your holes the purge fluid spates,
for crying out loud would you get a grip, let's stick to the present
and try to live there, or try to live here, just where is the present,
the present's complex, some days I think it's mostly a lie,
a faking embrace, how pushy we are to push ourselves forward,
Patty I'm leaving, I've had enough.

Western Tanager,
Golden-mantled Ground Squirrel,
Noah's stowaways.

Hey, Patty, I'm back, couldn't stay away, finally got as far
as the upper crater lake, snowmelt waterfall under the Divide,
high palisade, twelve thousand plus, this side of which it all goes to flow
Mississippiwise, soaked a battered toe there, it quickly went numb,
cupped a few mouthfuls without even purifying, hard to see what animals
would have laid waste in it, those mouthfuls were tough on sensitive teeth,
but the stinging was sweet because it was stolen, each icy swallow
picked the Gulf's pocket, kept back a little for one's private stash
from south forking creek, then from the confluence of south, middle, north,
then the Saint Vrain, that's a name, not a saint, into South Platte, the Platte
meets Missouri, Lewis and Clark, July 21st, 1804, today's the 16th,
with great veolsity rolling its Sands, found great dificuelty passing around
the Sand at the Mouth, then the Big River Twain has peed in, and finally
New Orleans, have a drink, altitude was altering, atmospheric pressure drops
as the bone-locker rises, oxygen wanes, we pant, breathe faster, heart rate up
but unlike with sex our chemistry hustles to adapt the blood, adjust it
more lastingly, up there overall mortality rate's lower, obesity too,
but before we sell out and move to high ground, let us consider
why people who live at great elevation take their own lives
at a rate that's higher and statistically significant, does higher mean lonelier,
are stars too bright, winter too long, beauty less bearable, safer to take
a cue from the athletes, train up there, high as you can, read, write, or think,
contemplate, pray, get used to breathing air that's thinner, then you descend,

join us down here for wear and tear, our fender benders, bumps and bruises,
your blood will be rich, you won't puff a bit, nothing will happen
that knocks the wind out of you, on the trip home, back of a shuttle bus,
three guys were gabbing, focused on football, maybe they're coaches,
their talk is so technical, one guy has printouts, is testing the others,
or maybe they're sportscasters, polo shirts with network logos,
or should it be Logos, when the bus stopped, I popped the question,
You guys coaches, No sir we're refs, professional refs en route
to ref school, classes, exams, never met professional refs, Thanks for doing
all that you do, I meant it too, they grinned at each other, Last time
we'll hear that, from here on out it's effing ref this and effing ref that,
that might look dated, hey future knowitalls, you smug condescenders,
you want to know us, you look it up, we worshiped this stuff,
poetry nothing, professional football, that's the true god, this isn't irony,
ask the bus driver, You like to watch preseason camp, No man, he said,
I like to see hitting, go ahead, chortle, or elevate an eyebrow,
this is what's real, this is our country, football widow my backside,
you see those gals go crazy in the stands, those were our maenads,
tear your eyes out, here comes Camilla, co-captain with Turnus,
one tit bared, women nonviolent, what are you smoking, as of last January
63 women await on death row, look it up, stare it down, so what,
that's only 2.02 percent of people on death row, well shityeah, nobody says
men are good, I'm only saying 63 women could take the big hit
for making big hits, let's go meet them, let's go get all 63 and make a raid
on something large, Navy Seals nothing, 63 Amazons with blood lust
    burning,
we could tear the tracks up, we could turn this thing around, read your Bible,
Jonathan and his armor-bearer, First Samuel 14, we're talking two,
count 'em two, ripped the Philistines' eyes right out, let's cut Philistines
a little bit of slack, I'm a Philistine too, think a woman can't kill, wake up,
and even if women kill less than men, they still kill themselves
at rates that keep rising, hear the father bewailing his child,
that is not a good sound, that is not birdsong, wood thrush, hermit thrush,
cerulean warbler, that will work the surplus talking off hefty hips,
make us forget about making a name, mountains out of mole hills,

well, hell, to a mole it is a mountain, a shiny-postcard snowy-bonnet
homicidal mountain, let's talk about mountains, those vertical oceans,
kill you in a second, get off the summit by noon, off its flanks by two,
lightning above tree line, it'll kick that well-toned gym ass
into the underworld, batting no eyelash.

Don't throw out a life
if someone else can use it.
Recycle insides.

Her heart now beats in someone else, her eyes look out of another head,
that's a tough one, sign up for transplant, chances depend on sudden death,
accident, suicide, the freest-range meat, Could a greater miracle take place
than for us to look through each other's eyes, Thoreau's gospel, chapter one,
how about this, what's the first question divinity asks, book of Genesis,
take a second, think it over, while you're thinking, let's check in
with Lewis and Clark, they're stuck waiting, May '06, for Rockies to melt,
that icy barier which seperates me from my friends and Country,
killing time on the upper Kooskooske, castrating stallions, racing horses
they haven't yet eaten, giving gifts, making trades, dispensing remedies
for simple complaints, easily relieved, independent of maney disorders
intirely out of the power of Medison, repeatedly noting separate lodges
for women sequestered in a certain situation, the Lewis periphrasis
straightens out Clark, a doghter now arrived at the age of puberty
who being a certain situation, eighty-five pages to go in the trip,
when it's all over, what'll we do, okay time's up, what's the first question,
Let there be light, that's not a question, not even half-credit,
here's the first question divinity asks, Yoo-hoo where are you,
yoo-hoo's been added to give it some bounce, lighten the serious,
still very serious, divinity doesn't require an answer, it only requires
we give the answer, I'm hiding here, Why are you hiding, I feel frightened,
maybe ashamed, Why feel frightened and maybe ashamed, it's a long story,
divinity says It's not a problem I've got all day, actually I have
all of your days, as long as it takes for you to come clean, say where you are,
then work on why, divinity uses first-person pronouns, at least in this skit,

but it doesn't have to, being divinity, the skit's just heuristic,
yet the question remains, where the heck are you and why do you hide there,
I haven't got a criminal record, background checks are breezes for me,
once over beers I asked a guy from the Secret Service, he had retired
so it was okay, do they have a file on me, he said I'll look, didn't even want
my social security, said don't insult me, next day he said you're so clean
my computer squeaked, so there you have it, nothing to hide
and yet I hide it, my nothing that is, why is that Patty, I hide behind you
and then behind you I hide behind words, the problem with hiding
full-time behind words, it doesn't take long to find they're small fig leaves,
too small for this junk, this package, this process, and mine's not so big,
words are small leaves, the longest are smallest, and then when the words
no longer answer, the quick wit and good manners of drawing you out
whoever you are, most of the time it does the trick to ask about you,
but when it all fails, I hide behind silence and fondle many teachings
about bridled tongues, I'm such a good hider I hope I can't find me.

My brother's keeper?
Because I have no brother,
I'll keep copperheads.

One could do better than be a keeper of copperheads, but how isn't clear,
high beams identify the pit viper body slurping across a steep mountain road,
should I gun over it, lessen the venom at large in the world, thirty feet more
suddenly he's custard, vultures will love it, some mouse will go free,
small bird, amphibian, nor is it clear what copperheads contribute,
certainly not beauty, even when lit with Full Thunder Moonlight
he's greasy, disgusting, yes I'm a mariner but not quite an ancient one
and blessings sometimes make me squeamish, the blesser blaspheming
with uppity presumption, how much could Coleridge know about snakes,
Britain has adders, but they're not aggressive, bite seldom fatal,
whereas copperhead males during the mating season, ooh baby watch out,
they also ambush, sink the fangs in, then they withdraw, let the juice work
and stalk the prey later, it seems we're agreed, full speed ahead
but I didn't do it, what a lame wuss, a pussy, a wimp, a ridiculous man

sadly unmanned, too much thinking, too many hours wasted imagining
how to whet another viewpoint, most of the guns recovered at Gettysburg
hadn't been fired, they were still loaded, those that were fired,
lots were shot high, officers testify, Cain slew Abel, that was the kickoff
and yet what it takes to kill gives the slip to many a human most of the time,
saving a killer, that's what perplexes, so is the timing of one's intervening,
psychomachia, one voice commanding Peace, Cush, come not between
the viper and its strike, the drunk and his drink, and yet intervention,
what commas do best, when to insert one, that's the next question,
Psalm 32, my strength was dried up as by summer heat, but cooler today,
wind turned around, now from northwest, from Lewis and Clark land,
out of the Rockies, it's not going well, they're stymied by snow,
friendly Chopunnish suggested they wait till Full Thunder Moon,
but if they delay, there's no getting back to the States this season,
June 10 they started, now the snow's got them, twelve feet, fifteen,
first time they retreat, if we proceed and Should git bewildered
the certainty was we Should lose all our horses consequently our baggage
also our enstrements our papers perhaps and thus we Should resque
the loss of our discoveries, first time they retreat, the party dejected,
but sometimes it's looney to push on ahead, no matter how demeaning
a retrograde motion, events intervene, this is the plan, it's a good plan,
but winter bombs away more snow than is usual, a mate behaves this way,
children make choices, pretty soon traction means backtracking, bub,
so shift to reverse and find a good guide, Lewis was a suicide
lots of people think, depressed heavy drinker, maybe malarial,
syphilitic perhaps, I fear the weight of his mind overcame him,
Clark said it best, quite a good mind, big mountains on it.

Retracing, he felt,
sad Lewis the Lewicide,
deeply mortified.

When an end comes in sight, it can encourage, won't be long now,
soon we can rest, put festered feet up, cherish achievement,
but sighting an end can also make tougher what's on in the meantime,
undermine focus imperative now, demands at hand just jealous enough

to henpeck hard a lapse in attention, give the strayed eye a nice tearful poke
for wandering away toward final destination, would somebody please
tell airline attendants that if it's not final it's not destination,
it's only a layover, way station, transfer, a passing punctuation
in the syntax of motion, Clark and his party are having a blast,
parting from Lewis at Traveler's Rest, the cache of tobacco
they buried last August dug up again, the boys chew and smoke,
first time in six months, then shoot down the Jefferson ninety-seven miles
first day out in dugouts they'd sunk, going at last with a downhill flow,
reaping excelsior the roundtrip reward, but Lewis is having a runt of a time,
he drew the wrong straw, sky is too cloudy for longitude reading
at camp disappointment, then as if fates were wholly against me
my chronometer stoped, next the Blackfeet who liked smoking pipes
tried stealing horses, also some guns, he had to shoot one
right in the belly, felt the warm wind from a bullet distinctly,
then he got shot clean through the left thigh, one of his men, blind in an eye,
took him for elk, my wounds very stiff and soar this morning
but gave me no considerable pain, what Lewis considers considerable pain
is nothing we want or could endure, someone like that, should he decide
he cannot stand living, take his word for it, don't intervene
or fret you should try, he's in a league we've never seen play.

Amorous armor
provides the best protection
with pure nakedness.

Good-byes have started, Colter has left, wanting to stay
to trap with two hunters, first whites they'd seen in more than a year,
first ones to follow the trail they'd made, can't hardly blame him,
what's in St. Louis after that trip, we were disposed to be of service
to any one of our party who performed as well, just like that
connection is severed, they settle with Colter, give him some powder,
then he's discharged, two years together, two years like those,
was there a bear hug, wet eye, some kidding, anything to ease
the strangling throat, or was it all business, a handshake, salute,
take care of yourself, drop us a line, then when they say

so long to the Snake Woman, her husband commanding
no language they needed, it was all we could do to get through the entry,
this is hard, Patty, this will be us, unlike Clark, the Red-Headed Chief,
I can't ever offer to take your son with me, butifull child, once he's weened,
and raise him the way I think is most proper, you cannot give me
powder and lead, things you don't want that may be of use,
clap my stiff back and wish me suckcess, separation anxiety,
when it's disorder, gets acronymed SAD, pretty good acronym,
if somewhat laconic, for psychopathology afflicting adults,
seven percent of us, emotional attachment, it can sneak up
and slip you its mickey, how does it work, spiking your life,
a few drops a day, when you look up, you're hooked by the gill,
anxious, see eager, its cinnamon synonym, but studious means eager,
is that all this is, this fondness for study, just a home remedy
for a bad case of SAD, today's August first, unusually cool
with heavy rain forecast, six weeks from today a year will have passed
since Patty and I began our self-helping, Lewis and Clark,
their trip took two years, two years and four months, and it was a failure
from one point of view, no way to canoe all the way west,
Thoreau at Walden, also two-plus, same length that Melville
got on and off whalers, grief takes two years, a shrink said so once,
she made a good case, first year you're reeling past first anniversaries,
a year ago this, a year ago that, each change of season a bruised souvenir,
big purple blooms on butterfly bushes, but then in year two
acute shades to chronic, that bottle of bereavement, been open a while,
had time to breathe, not great but it's drinkable, goes with most things,
something like braking distance, have to allow for how long it takes
to come to full stop, figure conditions, the weather, your speed,
Patty I'm moved to move that we quit, within the next month,
then I'll have time to sponge my spilled slaw before the next time
Antarctica sees moon shadow crossing its Earth share.

Hemophiliacs
need a midnight fox's bark
to thicken blood curds.

Still-life's a paradox, berries in bowls, verbena in vases, toss in a clock,
maybe a fox skull the dog has brought home, we get the point,
we're flibbertigibbets, fickle and fleeting, but oxymoronic, that's what it is,
to order these skins, arrangement preserves, tans the hide, salts the meat,
cans our tomatoes, it's all taxidermy, *ut pictura,* Life-Like Results,
All Species, Award-Winning, Visit Our Website, Where Quality Counts,
it's about walls, don't want to climb them so that's where we mount
permanent pictures of our impermanence, elk antlers deck the entrance hall
of Jefferson's villa, sent back by our boys, they've come upon whiskey,
first spiritious licquor in fifteen months, paintings and photographs,
diplomas, awards, oh yes and the books that bulge from clogged shelves,
taxidermatitis, what a condition, making arrangements, it's the main mania
no unguent assuages, but that's not the paradox, not the tough puzzle,
tougher one is that change doesn't change, perishing's imperishible,
abiding snapshots of what abides not, yep we get those till eye runneth over

(let's assess asses
on display while summer lasts,
aestival assets)

but where's a good likeness of infinite finitude, hard to frame that one,
we gave it a shot Patty, but one year won't do it, one life's too few,
we'd have to find someone to keep the thing moving, pick up the last line
right in the middle, if that's where we leave it, and carry it on,
sure we'd be gone, but that's not the point of the likeness we're lacking,
our dying we've done, done it to death, the likeness we lack has no Pacific
to reach and return from, one that would emulate the ongoing aggregate
of little oblivions, it doesn't matter what matter we're made of, watery flesh,
ocean receded, mountain eroded, even a universe in a universe series,
which this probably is, though how can we know, have to find someone
to keep making lines till that person dies, maybe mid-line, so on with others,
that's the one way, no not tradition, that's not the same thing,
tradition just means this is our club, you want to join, memorize password
and unsecret handshake, the menu of options, allusion buffet,
maybe we need many more poems, it isn't my call, but I'd like to see

a poem the end of I'll never see, a poem I'll help with, then I'll die during,
that would be likeness of what's going to happen, I'd even resign
all claim to copyright, give up signed authorship, forego awards,
just keep it moving, publish or not once I have perished, do it much better
and put me to shame, I'll tell you what, it's starting to rain,
forecast is calling for storms, some severe, I'm going to quit
and leave it right here, I thought I'd go on till a month from today,
but Patty let's kiss, I miss you already, my mouth to your   space bar,
oh leave the gap, our brand of lipstick, which you've never worn,
I can hear thunder, if caught in tornado look for a ditch, if caught
amidst lightning, not much you can do, a ditch full of water
could be your last bath, I'm off for a walk way up the mountain,
no kite in the sky, if I get struck, continue this line,